W9-CIC-440

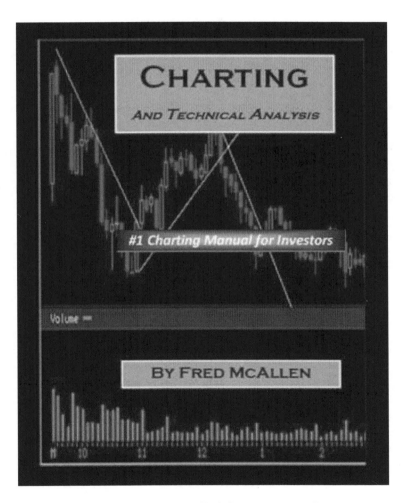

CHARTING

AND TECHNICAL ANALYSIS

#1 Charting Manual for Investors

Volume —

BY FRED MCALLEN

# Charting and Technical Analysis

2

# **Introduction**

Every investing mistake is a result of one thing. Either the wrong investment was purchased, or the investment was purchased at the wrong time. Historically, in good market times most every investment advances with the market. Even purchasing a bad investment during a strong bull market can sometimes be profitable. Yet during market declines, and especially in bear markets, the opposite holds true. During bad market times more than 80% of all stocks and funds decline in value.

Therefore, purchasing any investment at the wrong time is most always the recipe for loss.

Prior to every market decline, and particularly leading up to bear markets, there are market tops where unsuspecting and uninformed investors are continually sold investments that will certainly hand them a loss. Unfortunately, this is always a reoccurring tragedy. Since 1900 there has been a bear market on the average of every 3.5 years with an average decline of 29%.

Investing and trading can be profitable for the informed investor, but very costly for the uninformed.

One of the inspirations that led to writing this book came from a good friend with whom I had shared some of the techniques and strategies used in technical market analysis.

He later sent me the following message.

> *"Before I learned technical analysis, I was happy in my ignorance. I was not very profitable... but happy. But after learning the predictive value of charting, I could never feel safe in the market again without charts. It would be like driving cross-country without a road map. Charts really can tell you where to buy or sell and they have saved me from losses more times than I can count."*

Many in this generation have been led to believe that buy-and-hold is the ultimate in market knowledge. But, in today's markets, you need charting methods that have stood the test of time, and helped the informed investors navigate the treacherous trading and investing environment.

Throughout this book you will discover the difference between being informed and uninformed. You will become informed and learn to avoid making costly investing and trading mistakes.

*~Fred McAllen*

# Contents

 U.S. Government Required Disclaimer - Commodity Futures Trading Commission Futures and Options trading has large potential rewards, but also large potential risk. You must be aware of the risks and be willing to accept them in order to invest in the futures and options markets. Don't trade with money you can't afford to lose. This is neither a solicitation nor an offer to Buy/Sell futures or options. No representation is being made that any account will or is likely to achieve profits or losses similar to those discussed on this web site. The past performance of any trading system or methodology is not necessarily indicative of future results.

CFTC RULE 4.41 - HYPOTHETICAL OR SIMULATED PERFORMANCE RESULTS HAVE CERTAIN LIMITATIONS. UNLIKE AN ACTUAL PERFORMANCE RECORD, SIMULATED RESULTS DO NOT REPRESENT ACTUAL TRADING. ALSO, SINCE THE TRADES HAVE NOT BEEN EXECUTED, THE RESULTS MAY HAVE UNDER-OR-OVER COMPENSATED FOR THE IMPACT, IF ANY, OF CERTAIN MARKET FACTORS, SUCH AS LACK OF LIQUIDITY. SIMULATED TRADING PROGRAMS IN GENERAL ARE ALSO SUBJECT TO THE FACT THAT THEY ARE DESIGNED WITH THE BENEFIT OF HINDSIGHT. NO REPRESENTATION IS BEING MADE THAT ANY ACCOUNT WILL OR IS LIKELY TO ACHIEVE PROFIT OR LOSSES SIMILAR TO THOSE SHOWN.

# PREFACE

**Fire your Financial Advisor!**

Yes, that is a bold statement.

The primary objective in this book is to prepare you to take charge of your investment decisions by learning charting and technical analysis in detail.

But first, you need to know the cold-hard truth about investment firms and financial advisors. Only by understanding the truth, can you appreciate the importance of making your own investing decisions. So let's start there.

In today's world, the term 'Financial Advisor' means little or nothing. Unlike in years past when your investments were advised, made, and handled by a Stock Broker with years of experience under his belt, that is no longer the case.

The 'Modern Day Financial Advisors' are individuals being recruited from job posting sites like Monster and Hot Jobs by the investment firms in need of sales personnel. Yes, the major investment firms compete for what is referred to as "Assets under Management." And, in order to increase these assets, investment money must be placed with their firms. Your money.

To accomplish this all-important goal the investment firms must have sales personnel to actively sell investments to the public (you).

Here is where it gets interesting. These investment firms actively solicit sales people by listing job openings on the internet and also contacting unemployed persons who have posted a resume on the internet.

Now, in order for these new recruits to *legally* sell investments, they must first be licensed. This is easily accomplished by the investment firm purchasing a short online course for the new recruit, and then paying the fees to take the necessary exam. Once the recruit passes the exam, this person can now legally sell securities/investments.

This results in the first disturbing realization that in a matter of a few short weeks, an unemployed individual with absolutely no capital market or investment experience whatsoever suddenly becomes a licensed salesperson and *your* Financial Advisor.

**This person is responsible for making your investment decisions that will ultimately be your retirement.**

- ✓ Where is the knowledge?
- ✓ Where is the experience?
- ✓ Has this person ever bought or sold even *one* security?
- ✓ Your retirement depends upon this inexperienced individual and their lack of knowledge?

No, this is not something that just happens occasionally. The major investment firms turn out a new class of recruits every week.

Yes, you read that right. Every week, new recruits hit the streets supplied with a pocket full of brochures, a defined territory for neighborhood solicitation, a sales quota to meet, and a tablet computer to record any information you are willing to give them. Any information such as name, address, phone number, and hopefully an estimate of the dollar amount you might one day invest are dutifully recorded and the data is then linked to the investment firm's home office and stored for future contact, return visits, and sales.

The recruits do not have an office. If asked, they may say, "I am opening an office in the area." The extension of that lie is to tell you the company is currently working on lease arrangements or some similar fabricated story. The truth is, there is no office and there never will be an office unless and until the recruit meets a certain sales level for a predefined period of time. Thus, with enough sales, they can *qualify* for an office.

**I have been there and have witnessed it!**

*I have heard the instructors tell the new recruits:*

**"Just buy ONE share of an investment. Thus, when asked if the investment is 'safe,' you can assure the customer it is a safe investment, because you own it yourself."**

The advisor is not only trained to sell, they are under pressure to sell in order to meet sales quotas. Therefore, they will sell you something regardless what the market is doing or may be about to do. Many times the unsuspecting investor is advised to invest in whatever investment product is currently paying the highest commission, or whatever the investment firm may currently have in their inventory that they need to *unload*.

This is normally either mutual funds or annuities because commissions are too low on individual stock transactions for the salesperson to meet their defined sales quota. Another reason mutual funds are a high sales item is because they normally pay *trailing* commissions. This is part of the standard fees assessed by the fund and gives the recruit constant income rather than a one-time commission on a stock transaction.

Now, let's look at a couple of common sales tools used by investment salespeople and investigate the truth, or lack thereof.

## *Buy and Hold Theory*

This is one of the most popular arguments in the investing and trading world. Some investment firms use this theory as a sales technique to gain new investors; some will use this theory to convince their clients to hold on to a losing investment, some will use this theory to convince a disgruntled client to stay fully invested and hold their losses during a market downturn. The problem is, this theory is normally used for whatever purpose it might serve at the current time.

As an investor, you have to remember that new recruits are trained to sell. And, being a financial advisor is a sales job, so the need to sell never diminishes regardless how long an advisor has been selling. So convincing you to 'buy and hold' an investment is their top priority. Yet, for new recruits, there is no training on protecting your investment capital. And the same holds true for experienced advisors. Moving your money out of the market and into cash is not something any of them ever want to do.

Let's examine buy-and-hold a little closer. This theory has been around for years. In reality, yes, investing in stocks has *historically* averaged about a 10% per year return. That's what advisors will tell you, but let's take a closer look. Investment firms all have some wonderful chart to show you that holding an investment can be profitable. Most firms use what is called a *20-year rolling time period*. Meaning, investments held for 20 years have consistently been profitable. Why do you think '20' is the magic number? *Because anything less than 20 wouldn't work.*

You see, the market moves in trends and cycles. From 1982 – 2000 the market was in what is called a Secular Bull Market, meaning, a long-term bull market cycle. But prior to that, there was a Secular Bear Market from 1964 – 1982. Eighteen years of a sideways and declining market. For instance, in 1964 the Dow Jones Industrial Average was at 874. Seventeen years later at the end of 1982 it was at 875. Thus, investors who purchased investments in 1964 and held those investments more than likely, at best, broke even seventeen to eighteen years later. That's a long time to watch your investment dollars go absolutely nowhere.

Following the Secular Bear Market from 1964 to 1982, a new Secular Bull Market began. From 1982 to 2000 the market advanced for eighteen years. Thus, those buy-and-hold investors who got in the market in the early to mid sixties finally saw a return on their investment. And yes, anyone buying in near the bottom in the early nineteen eighties were handsomely rewarded as well. Since you probably know what happened to the market in 2000, you realize that 18-year Secular Bull Market came to a screeching halt.

The point being, advisors use a twenty-year rolling time period to sell you investments because twenty-year time frames allot enough time to get past an 18-year Secular Bear Market. What you need to remember from this little history lesson is this.

A Secular Bear Market has always followed a Secular Bull Market, and vice versa.

So regardless what sales presentation you are shown, it really does matter *when* you invest. You want to be getting in at the bottom, not the top.

So, what else is wrong with the buy-and-hold theory?

**It Depends upon 3 Things:**

1. How long you are able to hold your investment
2. When you purchased your investment
3. When you need to sell your investment

If you purchased your stocks, investment, or shares in a fund in let's say, 1950 and held them until 2007, then sold them at the markets' all-time-high. Yes! You would likely have made a 10% per year annualized return, maybe more. Would you be able to hold for long periods of time? Maybe. But since you don't receive 10% per year return on investment in dividends from the investment, you must rely upon the advance in the value of the fund or the individual company's worth, and subsequent increase in stock price to realize a 10% return on your investment.

Since you must depend upon the advance in stock price to realize the full potential of your investment, then:

- It not only depends upon *when* you purchased
- It also depends upon *when* you need to sell

This being the case: The *when* you purchased would need to be at a *low* point in the market, and/or stock price, and the *when* you sell would need to be at a *high* point in the market and/or stock price.
The point is:

The 'Buy and Hold' Theory is *only* correct under certain, and almost perfect conditions.

The investors who purchased stock in the late 1990s, early 2000, or 2007 at or near the high of the market and held their investments would wait for years to just break even. The investors who purchased stock in 1929 waited 25 years to break even. The market did not trade in net gain territory again until the mid 1950s. The same is true for those who purchased in the early 1960s. The market traded sideways until 1982.

Financial advisors may tell you that "Buy and Hold" is the way to invest. When presented with this theory – ask the advisor who purports such nonsense if the same advice was given to investors in 1929, or 1960, or 2000, or in 2007?

The truth is: During 1999, 2000, 2007, and anytime the market is advancing and many times approaching all-time highs, financial advisors continue to sell investments that will certainly lose. You cannot buy in at the market top and expect to make money.

When you invest, you *do not* know when you will need that money for a special circumstance and/or an emergency. You *do not* have the liberty of always choosing *when* you will sell and/or withdraw your funds to be used for other purposes. You may need your funds at a time when the prices are low, the market is in bear stages, or the economy is in a recession. Thus, a 10% return would be highly unlikely.

## Mutual Funds

One of the most popular investment vehicles is the mutual fund. A **mutual fund** is a professionally managed type of collective investment scheme that pools money from many investors and invests typically in investment securities such as stocks, bonds, short-term money market instruments, or even other mutual funds. The mutual fund will have a fund manager that trades (buys and sells) the fund's investments in accordance with the fund's investment objective.

You have likely been approached by the fund salesperson and shown all the different types of funds available, from conservative to aggressive.

Mutual funds have been around since the 1920s. But are they safe? Do they make money?

Realistically, not many of them make money. According to Morningstar who rates the funds as to their performance, 75% of funds with a 1 star rating in 2005 were wiped out over the ensuing 5 years. There are about 15,000 different funds, and only a handful consistently makes money for their investors, and finding the one that will make you money at any given time is like finding a needle in a haystack.

Look at it logically. How do mutual funds typically rate their performance? The performance of the S&P 500

Index is used as the industry standard benchmark to gauge the performance of mutual funds.

If the fund strives to beat the performance of the overall S&P 500, why not just invest your money in the S&P 500 index by buying shares of SPY? In doing so, you pay no fees to a fund, investment firm, fund manager, etc.

If you want to invest in a mutual fund, do your homework. Demand to see a performance of the past 5 years, and the past 10 years. See how the fund performed in bear market times and during recessions.

**Never rely on a Salesman for investment advice!**

In November 2007 I was invited to speak at a major investment firm's training center. There were 34 recruits in attendance that particular week from all over the United States. Prior to arriving, each recruit had been given six weeks to build a list of potential clients with a mandatory minimum of 25 per day, or 100 per week. Thus, every recruit had a minimum of 600 individuals to contact with hopes of selling an investment. So collectively, there were at least 20,400 potential sales. (34 recruits X 600 contacts) All recruits made sales calls while the instructors listened to the conversations and provided pointers on ways to improve their selling techniques. The recruits were provided three possible investments to sell depending on the potential client's interest.

1. A mutual fund
2. Shares of Pepsi stock
3. A bond in the firm's inventory

**VERY IMPORTANT:**

In November 2007, the market was near an all-time-high and topping out. Virtually every sale the recruits made resulted in either a loss to the investor, or the investor was forced to hold the investment for a long time in hopes of breaking even.

**Statistics:**

Here is another very troubling fact you should be aware of. During the last stages of the bull-market run in 1999-2000, the inflow of money to mutual funds was the highest level ever recorded. This same scenario repeated again in 2007, happening both times at the market tops.

Sure, uninformed investors were throwing their money in the market hoping for the advance to continue. But a Financial Advisor should have known better. They should have at least been suspect of a market top or correction. Yet, they continued to sell, and according to the statistics, they sold more than ever.

What happened next tells the rest of the story. Yes, the market entered a bear market and declined significantly, in the neighborhood of fifty percent. But that's only part of the story. During the bear markets of 2000 and 2007, investors were losing money and scared. The economic cycle went into recession. The Federal Reserve cut interest rates to help turn the economy around. Sales of mutual funds dropped because investors were no longer willing to throw money in the market. Some investors sold their shares and took their cash, and the loss. As you can imagine, during such times selling investments becomes extremely difficult. So what do Financial Advisors start selling? Bonds.

After interest rates are cut, bank certificates of deposit (CDs) are not paying much at all, if anything. So, financial advisors sell bonds. Corporate Bonds and Municipal Bonds usually pay better rates than a CD, so investors are convinced to move their money to a higher paying investment vehicle. It seems like a smart thing to do to move money from a CD that is paying nothing to a Bond that is paying a better return. What is wrong with this picture?

Well, you have to know how bonds are priced. Bond prices and interest rates are on an inverted scale. Meaning, as interest rates decline, bond prices increase. This is because the bonds that were issued and sold when interest rates were high are more valuable as interest rates decline. Simply put, you would pay more for a bond that was yielding 6% return than you would pay for one yielding 2% return. So those bonds paying a higher return suddenly become more expensive.

Yes, a Bond that was issued while interest rates were high becomes more valuable as interest rates decline, and on the flip side of that coin, bonds purchased while interest rates are low will become less valuable as interest rates inevitably increase.

So the bottom line is; Financial Advisors sell bonds when they can't sell other investments, and they sell them at the wrong time. Every bond sold while interest rates are low will either require the investor to hold the bond until maturity for whatever return it is paying, or sell the bond for a loss as the interest rates move higher. In other words, bond investing is backwards from stock investing. You don't 'buy low – sell high' like you do with stocks. You want to buy bonds while rates are high and sell when rates are low. So yes, in essence you 'buy high – sell low.'

As you can see, some investors can be hit with a double loss. As the stock prices and fund values decline, they then move their money to the safety of bonds, then as interest rates are raised, they can experience another loss because the value of their bonds decline.

## Dollar-Cost-Average

Here is another sales technique Financial Advisors use to coax the unsuspecting public into investing their hard-earned money. Dollar-Cost-Averaging is when you allocate money to invest each month and deposit a specific amount in an investment account. It's a novel idea, but if you are going to do it, then you should start at the bottom, not the top. You should never make the mistake of buying at the top and adding to positions all the way down. Sure, in theory you would be doing this over a period of many years, buying when prices are low and when prices are high thus, averaging in to your positions.

The truth is, if you start buying at the top, at the beginning of a bear market, then you will be adding to a losing position for about two years. Yes, I will mention 'bear markets' several times throughout this book, and that's okay. Because recognizing bear markets and appreciating and respecting their devastation is one of the most important things you can learn.

To summarize, you are the only one that has any control of your financial future. A financial advisor is not your friend. They are in sales. Your financial future depends upon your knowledge, and you don't want to be sold an investment at the wrong time. By the end of this book you will be knowledgeable in making decisions on when to invest and when to keep your hard-earned cash in your pocket. That is ninety percent the battle. You will learn how to do it right, and how to protect your capital.

## Everyone is a trader

You may initially disagree with that statement, but it's true. Common sense tells us that if you were certain that the market was about to enter a major decline, you wouldn't run to your broker's office and buy a truckload of stocks. You wouldn't log on to your online trading account and load up on the stock de jour, which would be whatever stock the TV talking heads were pushing that day.

No, every investor makes a conscious decision to enter the market when they believe they will make money, not lose it. So in reality, everyone is a trader.

Whether you are a short-term trader or a long-term investor, predicting what you believe the market as a whole, or the future price of an individual stock or security may be is paramount in whether you are successful or not. All traders and investors are the same. They expect to make money.

## Price forecasting

Since we are all traders, price forecasting is usually the first important step in our decision making process. With every investment, the investor obviously must conclude in some way as to the reason to purchase. Obviously believing the price will increase in order to reap the reward from the increase in the form of profit. Price forecasting entails far more than a blind theory, or a hot tip from someone at the water fountain.

Determining the risk versus reward ratio for each investment requires looking at the past price movement to help us reasonably conclude where the price may be in the future. By looking where something came from, we have a better picture as to where it is headed.

Price forecasting, however, is only the first step in the decision-making process.

## Market Timing

The second, and often the more difficult step is *market timing.*

For short-term traders, minor price moves can have a dramatic impact on trading performance.

For long-term investors, the aspect of market timing is just as important. You should never simply buy a stock or mutual fund 'willy-nilly' at whatever price it might be presently selling for, using the excuse that you are going to be holding it long term, so a few dollars doesn't matter. As you have hopefully learned by now, a few dollars can turn into a complete disaster.

Need I remind you that purchasing a DotCom stock in 1999 with the intent to hold it long term may have sent you to the bankruptcy court instead of comfortable retirement. Yet, when I generalize that statement by using the term DotCom, you should not think that *only* refers to some fly-by-night company that never made any money and went bankrupt when the 'Bubble' burst. What if you had purchased a company like Intel or Microsoft? Both of which are huge companies and components of the thirty stocks that make up the Dow Jones Industrial Average. These too, were selling at a price more than three times the price they sold for more than 10 years later.

Therefore, the precise timing of entry and exit points is an indispensable aspect of any trade, short term or long term. To put it bluntly, *timing is everything* in the stock market. For reasons that will soon become apparent, timing is almost purely technical in nature. This being the case, the application of charting principles becomes absolutely essential at some point in the decision making process.

The success of your financial future is greatly enhanced by your ability to view the overall picture of the market and reasonably conclude a direction. For instance, is it likely the market is heading up, or down? In doing this, *never* falsely assume that whatever stock you might be holding or be interested in will increase in value regardless what the overall market does. Always remember: "All ships rise or fall with the tide."

This is so true with stocks. It doesn't matter if you own stock in the strongest company on the planet or the best performing Mutual Fund on earth, if the overall market drops; the value of your investment will follow the overall market most every single time.

With this in mind, possessing the knowledge to correctly ascertain *general market* movement, and reasonably predict *future market* movement, are key factors for your success.

Charting, and interpreting the information on a chart is the only way to reasonably predict the future direction of the market. Nothing else will allow you to do that. Regardless how long you study the financials of a company or the economic outlook of the economy, you won't find the information a stock chart will tell you.

That's why it is imperative to learn to apply charting analysis to both short-term and long-term trading and investing.

**Educate yourself! Let's get started.**

# CHAPTER 1

## *The Dow Theory*

-

Technical Analysis has some very solid roots, The Dow Theory. From 1900 to the time of his death in 1902, Charles Dow wrote a series of editorials published in The Wall Street Journal regarding his theory of the stock market. Dow believed the stock market was a barometer of the overall health of the economy, and, he believed the stock market moved in predictable ways. He felt that if the economy was advancing, then the stock market would reflect the healthy economy with advancing prices in stocks. Similarly, in a contracting economy, he believed the stock prices would reflect that as well.

Dow created what we know today as the Dow Jones Industrial Average, a select list of eleven large companies that encompassed a wide range of business areas. His theory was that the health of these companies would mirror the health of the economy, and, as these company's output and revenues changed, then the economy would change as well. Today there are thirty companies that make up the DJIA, from banking to health care, manufacturing, retail, and technology.

Charles Dow was right. We see it today as clearly as he saw it more than one hundred years ago. The market truly is a barometer of the economy. The market does, and has always moved in predictable ways. When company revenues, earnings and output begin to contract, the economy is either already contracting or is not far behind. And, as companies begin to expand, the economy follows.

I'm sure you have read about market 'indicators.' The news is always mentioning one indicator or another, trying to determine what is going to happen in the future. There are housing prices, home sales, jobless rates, employment activity, and any number of indicators used to keep a close eye on the health of the economy. Why? It's simple… As the economy goes, so goes the stock prices. What's more important is this. As an 'indicator,' the Dow Jones Industrial Average is a 'leading indicator' as to what is about to happen in the economy.

The stock market has always begun to move higher about six months before a recession is officially over. And, it has always begun to drop and contract about six months before a recession begins. Again, Charles Dow was right; it is our leading indicator, our window to the future, so to speak.

Learning the movements of the overall market is a very important part of investing and trading. As you will learn, if you invest or trade against the market, or its trend, you will lose. It does not matter how much you love a particular stock, index, or mutual fund. If the overall market goes down, then so will your investment. Some believe that perusing the financials of companies to find the strongest balance sheets is the best way to invest, picking those with a stellar bottom line. Need I remind you of MCI or Enron? Even by excluding the crooked companies who cook their books, great companies still follow the overall market. Their stock prices will rise and fall with the overall market every time.

**"All ships rise and fall with the tide."**

First, let's look at how the overall market consistently and predictably moves in patterns and trends. This is one of the most important factors in trading and investing. You must always invest and trade with the market, not against it.

## The Dow Theory's Basic Premise

"The Market Discounts Everything"

The stock market being a barometer of the economy's health is only one aspect of the Dow Theory. A basic premise of the Dow Theory is, 'the market discounts everything.'

Meaning, all information - past, current, and even future - is discounted into the markets and reflected in the prices of stocks and indexes.

That information includes everything from the emotions of investors to inflation and interest-rate data, along with pending earnings announcements to be made by companies after the market close. (Note: Companies do not announce earnings reports while the market is open for trading. Companies announce earnings reports either before the market opens or after the close of the market.)

Thus, the only information excluded from the current market prices is that which is unknowable, such as a massive earthquake or possibly a terrorist attack. But even then the risks of such an event are priced into the market. And no, this does not mean that market participants or the market itself can somehow predict future events. But it does mean that over any period of time, all factors - those that have happened, are expected to happen, and could happen - are priced into the market.

I am certain you are aware that on any given day the market fluctuates up or down based on numerous factors. It may rise because the unemployment rate dropped, indicating a healthy and stable economy, or it may fall because of some other factor. The main point you must remember when you see this happening on a daily basis is the market is discounting whatever the news may be at that moment. As things change, such as market risks, economy, interest rates, or whatever, the market adjusts along with the prices, reflecting that new information.

To apply this to technical analysis today, we need only look at price movements, and not at other factors such as the balance sheet of a company. Just like mainstream technical analysis, Dow Theory is mainly focused on price and volume, because the stock price of a company is reflecting what the balance sheet of the company suggests.

Therefore, I don't have to try to figure out the accounting wizardry of a company to determine whether to buy the stock or not. All I have to do is look at the stock's price and volume, and, know how to interpret that information.

Another premise of the Dow Theory that we will use in our technical analysis is the market moves in trends. Let's look at the Three-Trend Market.

## *The Three-Trend Market*

Before we trade or invest in any stock, or even a market index or a mutual fund, we want to know the overall direction of the market. Dow recognized the market moves in trends and cycles, much like the overall economy. The Dow Theory says there are three trends to market movement.

1. **Primary trend**
2. **Secondary trend**
3. **Minor trend**

In the following chart we can see all three of these trends.

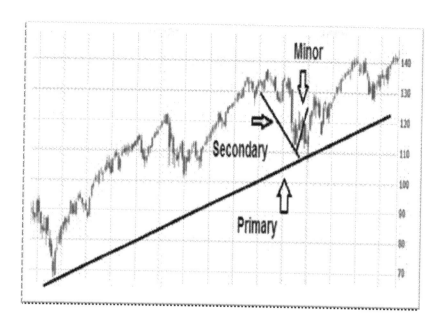

The primary movement is what its name suggests, primary. This is the overall direction on a longer term basis. Yet during an overall advance, there are secondary trends in the opposite direction, shorter time periods where the market pulls back. These declines are within the overall advance, and even within these declines, or pullbacks, there are minor trends.

We see in the following chart that the same is true in a declining market.

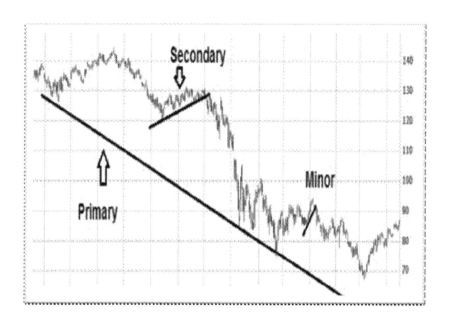

As I've already said, the market discounts everything, it fluctuates, and during this process, it does not move in a straight line whether the overall market is advancing or declining. It is going to zig-zag, so when placing your money in the market, you must know what the primary trend is. The primary trend is the most important of the three trends. It is the granddaddy of the three trends, and will dictate whether you make money or not.

If you ignore the primary trend, you are most likely going to lose money. The only time you should be buying stocks, index funds, or mutual funds is when the primary trend is advancing. But even then, you want to get in on the early stages of the advance. You don't want to be the last one to the party.

# Determining the Trend

Determining a trend in the market is quite simple. We want to know if the market is advancing (uptrend) or declining (downtrend).

## Uptrend

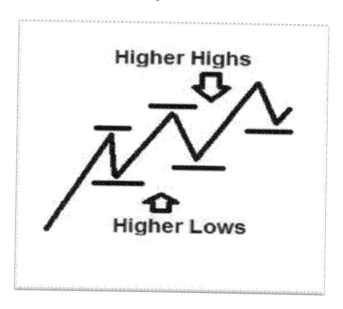

The chart above shows that during an advance, or uptrend, each small advance pushes higher, so there are continued higher highs. We call each high a 'peak.' During an uptrend the lows, we call the valleys, are higher as well. Each time the market pulls back, it does not go as low as it did the previous time and then makes a higher high.

## Downtrend

During a downtrend, or decline in the market the opposite is true. Each high is followed by a lower high, and each low is followed by a lower low.

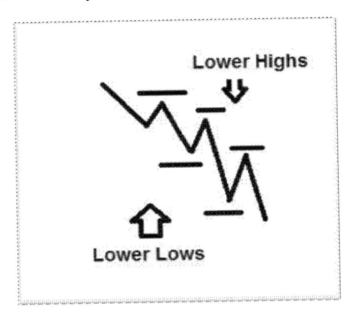

Simply by pulling up a long-term chart of the DJIA or the S&P 500, the primary trend is fairly easy to see.

After you first determine the primary trend, and it is advancing, then you can wait for a pullback (secondary trend) to buy your investment.

Determining the overall market trend is imperative. The Dow Theory teaches that once a primary trend is in place, it continues until something forces it to change. It is much like Newton's Law. "An object moves at a constant velocity, unless acted upon by a force."

Once a primary trend, either uptrend or downtrend, is in place, it tends to continue until something causes it to change. That may be a recession after a long uptrend, or a reaching a support level after a long downtrend.

Most financial advisors are not going to miss a sale and will take your money any day of the week. They won't tell you the market is possibly headed into a long-term decline, such as a bear market. Those declines are what will send you to the poor house, especially if you bought in close to the market top. It is up to you to determine when it is a good time to put your money at risk and enter the market.

With that said, let's take a closer look at the granddaddy of trends and see how the primary trends change and how those changes are actually phases in a market cycle.

# CHAPTER 2

## *The Three Phases of Primary Trends*

Since the most important trend to recognize is the primary trend, this leads into the third premise of the Dow Theory. Dow recognized there are three phases to every primary trend.

1. **The Accumulation phase**
2. **The Public Participation phase**
3. **The Distribution phase**

We can see these phases on the following chart.

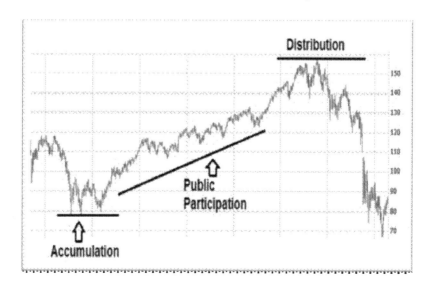

Let's take a look at each of the three phases as they apply to both bull and bear markets.

## *The Accumulation Phase*

In the preceding chart we see after the market sold off and finally reached a low, it traded higher two times only to fall back again. We will discuss this accumulation phase more in later chapters, but for now, you need to recognize what Charles Dow was referring to. You can see that after a sell-off, after the market has been in a decline for an extended period of time, the prices bottom out. This happens after a major market correction, such as a bear market. This is when the smart money enters the market and starts buying the discounted stocks, accumulating, and positioning in preparation for the next advance.

The first stage of a new bull market is referred to as the accumulation phase. To get you to thinking market psychology a little, try to imagine after a considerable sell-off, the buyers that step back in to pick up the bargains are the Pros. They have seen this type of market action before and recognize the stock prices are 'on sale' so to speak. They are normally the ones buying in the Accumulation Phase. No, they didn't dollar-cost-average all the way down as the market kept declining; they didn't buy in at the previous market top and sell out at the bottom. No, they were sitting on the sidelines with cash in hand waiting for the market to hit bottom. Once it became reasonably apparent the bottom was in place, that the risk of further decline was minimal, and the chance of a future advance was very good, then, and only then, did they risk their money. Do you see the risk/reward ratio here? Risk your money when the risk is low and the reward is high.

Baron Rothschild, the 18th century British nobleman and member of the Rothschild banking family, is credited with saying:

**"The time to buy is when there's blood in the streets."**

That might be a slight exaggeration, but really not that far from the truth. Experienced investors who have been in and around the market for many years tend to sit on the sidelines and simply watch the market. They wait for the most opportune time to enter, times when the risk/reward factor is heavily in their favor.

You must be the same way. Don't be chasing the market, buying in after a long-term advance. Ignore what the talking heads blather about on TV. There will always be someone either writing articles or smiling in front of a camera claiming the market is going to go higher. The more times you hear this – the more suspicious you should be.

**"You can always find someone who will give you enough rope to hang yourself."**

## *The Public Participation Phase*

As the accumulation phase materializes, a new primary trend moves into what is known as the Public Participation Phase. This phase is usually the longest lasting of the three phases. This is also the phase you want to be invested in, an advancing market.

During this phase, earnings growth and economic data improve and the public begins to tip-toe back into the market. As the economy and the related news improve, more and more investors move back in, and this sends stock prices higher.

As you can see in the previous chart, during the Public Participation Phase, the market experiences a long-term advance while the primary trend moves higher with secondary trends (pull-backs) along the way. These advances can last several years. Historically, there is a bear market on the average of every three and one-half years. Therefore, an advancing bull market should last around three years before another bear market begins.

This is where you should realize that it is very important as to when you invest, especially if you are tempted to do dollar-cost-averaging. Bear markets historically last 1.7 years, meaning the market declines during that time, so the primary trend would be down. It then takes another 1.5 years for the market to get back to break-even status. Thus, if you began buying in at the top and purchased all the way down, then you could be losing money for several years before ever seeing a point where you broke even.

## The Distribution Phase

The third phase is the distribution phase. This phase is the one that seems to always catch investors and traders unaware. The market has been in an advancing primary trend, and many think it will continue to move higher. But take another look at the chart.

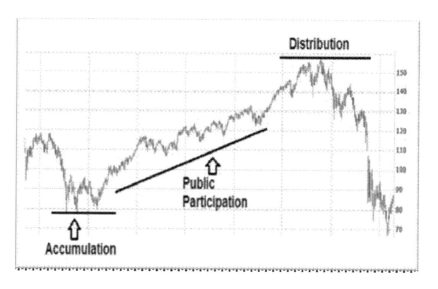

Dow correctly named this phase because of the trading activity going on during this phase. Remember the smart money buyers who were 'accumulating' during the accumulation phase, buying while there was blood in the streets? They are the ones selling in the distribution phase. The investors and traders that are often caught unaware are the ones normally doing all the buying during the distribution phase, buying from the smart money investors and traders.

Some say it is harder to call a market top than a market bottom. That is somewhat true. But a market top always has certain characteristics that can be recognized.

Market tops form after a long advance. The market seems to get tired and stops advancing and begins moving sideways.

The market stops making new highs. It no longer has the momentum to push higher, so it starts trading sideways and then begins to 'roll over.'

Volume dries up. We will discuss trading volume in later chapters, but at market tops, the heavier volume trading days are days when the market is selling off, closing lower. On days when the market moves back up, the volume is light. This tells you that the big money is not buying. They may not be selling, but they aren't buying. They may be waiting for the opportune time to sell.

Margin debt reaches extremely high levels. That's right, historically the market tops out and starts heading down when everyone is 'in.' In 1929 people would borrow money to buy stocks; some even borrowed against their home. During the last few market tops the margin debt was at nose-bleed levels. Investors and traders were borrowing against the stock they already owned to buy more stock. Not a smart thing to do, but they believed the hype that the market would continue to go higher and they became greedy wanting to make more money.

Euphoria. Euphoria is another characteristic of a market top. I'm sure you can remember when the internet bubble was about to implode. There were wild claims that stock prices were going much higher, analysts were issuing strong-buy recommendations on stock of companies that had never turned a profit, margin debt was at all-time high levels, and this list could go on and on.

Over a century ago, Jesse Livermore, probably the best trader of all time, said, "Nothing ever changes."

He was right. That was true in 1929 right before the crash and every market top since that time, including 2000, 2007, and every subsequent market top that will catch investors unaware.

That is classic for the Distribution Phase of a market cycle. John Q. Public, the small investor is buying and the Rothschilds of the world are selling to him. That is why this phase is so accurately named. Stocks are being 'distributed' out of the hands of the Pros and into the hands of the small investor who is unaware and will suffer the loss when the market declines.

As we look at charts in later chapters you will see how the accumulation and distribution phases of the market recognized by Charles Dow are very apparent in today's market. These phases are a part of every market cycle.

# *Three Phases in a Declining Market*

The three phases of a market cycle change very little during a declining market. The Distribution phase is always at the top and the Accumulation Phase is at the bottom. The Public Participation Phase still resides in the middle, but normally does not cover as long a time frame as it does during an advancing market.

We will discuss market trends in later chapters, but for now, notice on the left side of the above chart that I included the previous Primary Trend. That trend was broken when the market failed to make higher highs and began trading sideways during the Distribution Phase.

The Public Participation Phase is a little different during a declining market. Looking back at the chart for an advancing market you see the public kind of tip-toes into the market and the advance is gradual and takes a bit longer to materialize. Conversely, in a declining market you can see the steep drops in the above chart where the public was exiting the market quickly as their losses mounted. That is normally the case. As the market continues to drop more and more investors and traders throw in the towel, take their loss, and lick their wounds.

At the end of the Public Participation Phase, there is always an Accumulation Phase. The experienced investors, who recognized the previous market top, knew the market was not likely going any higher, and sold during the Distribution Phase start stepping back in. They scoop up the bargains and position themselves for the next market advance. Many of them have been sitting on the sidelines holding their cash and waiting for the market to reach a bottom. They only buy when the risk is low and the reward is high.

To them, these market phases are nothing new. The market has been moving through these same phases for more than a century. Charles Dow recognized it in 1900, and nothing has changed since that time.

# CHAPTER 3

# THE LAWS OF CHARTS

## *"Charts are the Footprint of Money"*

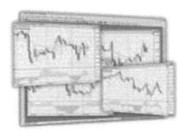

## *Technical Analysis Today*

Successful participation in the financial markets demands some mastery of chart analysis. Consider the fact that all decisions in various markets are based, in one form or another, on a market forecast. That is exactly what Charles Dow had the vision to recognize and created a way to implement such a forecast more than 100 years ago. It still holds true today.

There are many different types of traders with just as many different trading styles and strategies. There are only a selective number of investors who do not use charts. These non-charting types are all about the numbers. Their belief is that all investment decisions should be based solely on the company earnings, profit loss ratios, price earnings (P/E) ratios, etc. They enjoy looking at, and crunching the numbers.

The problem with this is if you rely only on fundamentals, you never know whether you have all the necessary facts to make an informed judgment. Some are purposely hidden, withheld, or delayed. Others just may not come to your attention. You have to read everything in sight to make sure that you are not missing a "revised estimate of earnings," or a news story about the books being *cooked*, the loss of a government contract, or news about the order backlog or a contract cancellation.

And if you use the Internet for research, false rumors are intentionally circulated to enable the criminals to capitalize on the reaction to rumors. So for all intents and purposes, a fundamental approach is severely limited at best.

## Why are Charts so important?

One thing to always remember is - *the charts don't lie.* The charts represent the money on the table at the end of the day. That is why they are of major importance.

The beauty of technical analysis is that it is 'scam proof.' It relies on your ability to read the charts and the price data, not on public or insider information. With the technical approach, you know that what you know about a specific index reading is all there is to know. There is no more. If there was anything else to know, the price would have already changed to discount that new information. Nobody can con you and you can be sure nothing has gotten by you. The price is the price. Follow the money.

Although I certainly see the benefits of number crunching, I also believe "A picture is worth a thousand words." Furthermore, I don't like spending my time, and I don't suspect you as a reader have the time to analyze the quarterly statements, inventory reports, sales reports, etc, of each company that you might want to trade or invest in.

Charts are a widely used tool in trading and investing to quickly see the past performance of the stock, the highs, the lows, trends, moving averages, trading volume, and much more.

Charts really are the 'footprint of money.' What some talking head on a financial news network might say becomes immaterial when you can look at a chart and see what the 'money' is saying. That's what is important. Seeing the money on the table and understanding by the propensity of evidence who was buying and selling and how serious they were.

It is also very true that 'history repeats itself.' Meaning, if a stock has historically been unable to penetrate a resistance level on the upside, then there is a reasonable probability that it will repeat that problem again. And looking at the flip side of that scenario, if the stock has historically held at a support level during a decline, and refused to fall farther, then there is the same reasonable probability that it will repeat that in the future.

As we progress, remember, when looking at charts and chart patterns, the chart shown in each figure will be of one stock or index in particular. However, the same information you learn regarding any chart we are discussing, will apply to *any other* chart on any other company, and/or index. The patterns, the candles, the volume, and every other aspect of one chart will apply to others as well.

## *Charts in Detail*

We will start with a single Line Chart and Bar Chart and progress from there.

A single line connecting successive closing prices is the simplest form of charting. These line charts are useful for trend analysis going back 2 – 5, or even 10 years or more.

See Figure 3 below.

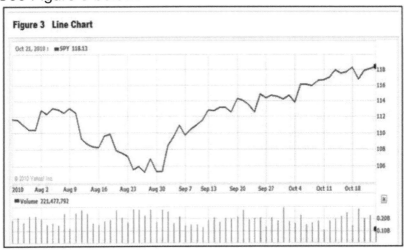

**Figure 3   Line Chart**

The chart below is a bar chart and is one of the most basic forms of charting. Even in its simplicity, we can determine the general movement of the stock, and draw a reasonable conclusion as to the possibility of future movement.

See Figure 3-2 below.

# Charting and Technical Analysis

Analysis

**Figure 3-2**

As you can see, the stock was trading in December (center of the chart) in the $35 to $40 range and over the course of 6- months it doubled in price. This was obviously during the tech boom of the late 90s or early 2000. Thus, over a 6-month period of time, the primary trend was up.

Note that each day in the above chart is indicated by a separate 'bar.' Each bar has a little **'tick'** on the left side indicating the opening price that day, and the little **'tick'** on the right side of the bar indicated the closing price for that day. The length of the bar tells us the trading range for that particular day, as noted by the arrows on the above chart. Here is a closer look at how the daily bars on a chart indicate the opening price, the closing price, and the trading range for the day.

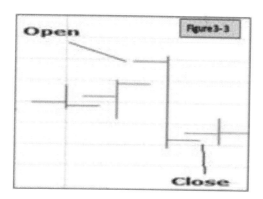

Remember this as we progress.

Also remember that whether you are looking at a daily, hourly, or even a weekly chart, the trends and pattern formations will tell you pretty much the same thing in relation to the chart you are viewing. Meaning, if you are looking at a daily chart, then the general trend should be viewed as a daily basis. In other words, do not make decisions for long-term investments based on what you see on a 5-minute chart or an hourly chart. And don't make day-trading decisions based solely on a one year chart.

For instance: A 3-month chart shows the daily bars for each trading day represented on that chart. And, a chart of one single trading day will show 1-minute, 5-minute, or possibly 10-minute bars. But each bar represents its open, close, and the trading range for its respective time period.

The construction of a daily bar chart is simple. Fortunately, these are free on the Internet, and constructed for you. The vertical bar is drawn from the day's high to the low. The tick to the left is the opening price that day; the tick to the right is the closing price.

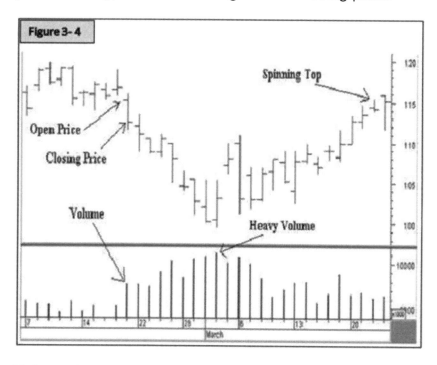

Figure 3- 4

Volume bars are drawn along the bottom of the chart. See these indicated by the arrows on the above chart. These are very important indicators, and we will be discussing volume later.

Price plotting is an extremely simple task. The daily bar chart has both a vertical and horizontal axis. The vertical axis (along the side of the chart) shows the price scale, while the horizontal axis (along the bottom of the chart) records calendar time. The first step in plotting a given day's price data is to locate the correct calendar day. This is accomplished simply by looking at the calendar dates along the bottom of the chart. Plot the high, the low, the opening, and closing (settlement) prices for the market. A *vertical bar connects the high and low* (the range). The *closing price* is recorded with a horizontal tick to the right of the bar. (Chartists mark the *opening price* with a tick to the left of the bar.) For each day, simply move one step to the right. *Volume* is recorded with a vertical bar along the bottom of the chart.

As I said, these are constructed for you, but it is vitally important that you understand what each bar and their respective ticks mean. These will be used in detail as we progress.

Another type of charts, are the candlestick charts. Although the basic information is the same as the bar chart, they are widely used because of their ease in quickly determining the information.

The following is a daily candlestick chart of Intel covering two months. Candlestick charts are preferred by some because the view is easier to see the color variations indicating up and down days.

See Figure 3-5 below.

## Candlestick style chart

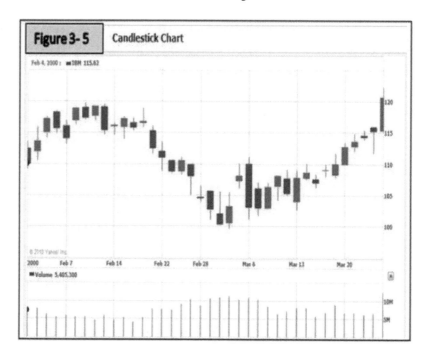

**Figure 3-5** | Candlestick Chart

The narrow wick of each candle is the day's trading range. The fatter portion, the body on the candle, is the area between the opening price and the closing price. Open candles are positive, meaning the stock closed at the top of the open body. This is the same as the bar chart showing the 'Tick' on the right side of the bar as the closing price. The darker candles are negative, meaning the stock closed at the bottom of the body. In other words, it opened higher for that day and fell to close at a lower price.

Let's look at the difference in bar charts and candlestick charts. Candlestick charting gives exactly the same information as the bar chart as you can see in the following picture; the candlestick is more colorful and easier to quickly assess the information.

The following is a comparison of Candlestick vs. Bar Chart.

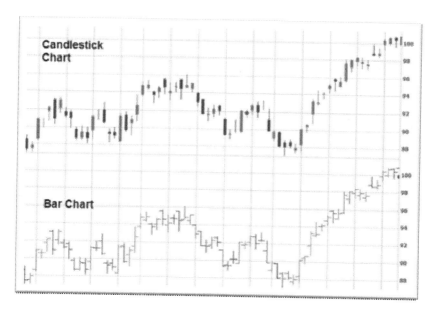

Some prefer one, some prefer the other. The two charts say the same thing – they just simply look different. So use whichever one you personally prefer.

# CHAPTER 4

## *Candlesticks Defined*

### What does the *Candlestick* look like?

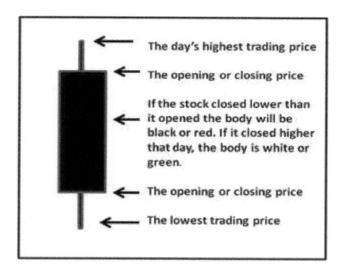

What does **Red (or Black) Candlestick** Mean?

The color of the candlestick tells us whether that candle was formed by a positive trading day (advance in price) or a negative day (decline in price). If the closing price is lower than the day's opening price, then the body of the candle is red or black. See following picture.

The day's highest trading price

The opening price

The closing price

The lowest trading price

**NOTE:** Most charting software allows you to customize your charts to reveal your desired colors. This enables you to choose your personal preference as to the color for your OPEN candles and for the CLOSED candles.

How about the *White Candlestick?*

The white candle, also known as the "OPEN" Candlestick, shows the price has moved up. Candlesticks will have a body and usually two wicks on each end. The bottom of the white body represents the opening price and the top of the body represents the closing price. The top and bottom tips of each wick are the day's highest and lowest price respectively.

Thus, this candle will represent a positive "CLOSE".

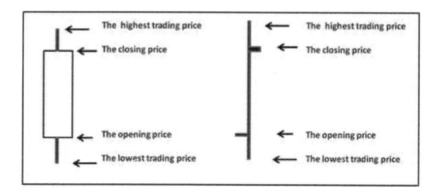

In the preceding comparison, you can see that the Bar and Candlestick charts would say the same thing. They simply look different.

Let's look at some very familiar 'indicators.' Candlesticks form based solely on the price movement and many of the candles are very telling. They are great indicators of what is likely to happen in the near future with respect to the price of the stock. Many of these candles have been given names to identify them. So let's look at each one and learn the importance it has when seen on a chart.

## The ALL IMPORTANT DOJI!

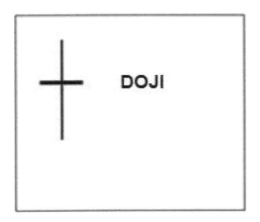

DOJI is a name for candlesticks that form when a stock's opening price and closing price are virtually equal. This DOJI tells us that during the trading day the stock moved higher and lower and neither the buyers nor sellers were more prominent. It says the stock traded up and the sellers stepped in and traded lower and the buyers stepped in. When just looking at a DOJI it appears very uneventful, but when combined with other candles and trends, it can be very telling.

When thinking in the perspective of a market trend moving higher or a downward trend moving lower, the DOJI is a very telling sign that the number of buyers and sellers has become equal. Therefore, after the market or stock has been in a trend, either up or down, and suddenly a DOJI is formed, then this tells us that since the buying and selling has equaled out – then a reversal of the current trend may be ahead. We will see and discuss the DOJI quite often as we progress.

## The Shooting Star

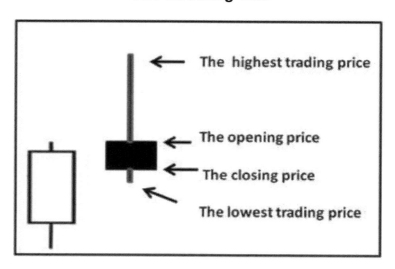

The highest trading price

The opening price

The closing price

The lowest trading price

The Shooting Star is a Bearish candle that forms after an advance in the stock or index price. Try to think of it in this manner. The price has advanced for several candles, or days, and tries to continue the advance. It opens and trades higher, creating the tall wick on top of the candle, but then the sellers take over forcing the price back down to close near the opening price. This is an early indication that the advance has lost its momentum. Technically, according to the above picture, the closing price would need to be below the opening price. However, that is not always the case. Meaning, if you simply switched the open and closing prices on the above picture, it would still indicate an early warning for a reversal, maybe just not as pronounced as the close that is lower than the open. But it would still be a warning sign.

## The Evening Star

This is also a bearish candlestick pattern that forms after an advance in the stock price. By itself, the DOJI at the top of the formation would just be a DOJI, meaning the opening and closing prices were virtually equal. But when the dark candle forms the following day indicating a change in direction, then this DOJI becomes what is called an Evening Star.

The formation shown by the chart above is used by traders as an early indication that the uptrend is about to reverse.

The large white candle preceding the DOJI indicates buyers jumping in *after* a significant advance. The Evening Star indicates inability to move higher, and the

Bearish Engulfing candle the following day confirms the sellers have entered the market.

Another very important Candle is called the Hammer.

## The HAMMER

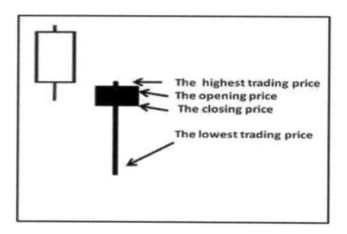

The **Hammer** is normally found at the bottom and forms when a stock has been in a downtrend and finally reached a support level. The formation of the hammer occurs when a security trades significantly lower than its opening price, but rallies later in the day to close either above or very close to its opening price. This pattern forms a hammer-shaped candlestick. It is very similar to a mirror image of the Shooting Star at the top of an advance.

When this Candle forms at the top of a pattern after an advance, it is called the Hanging Man. Both look very similar and can have either a positive or negative body.

## The *Hanging Man*

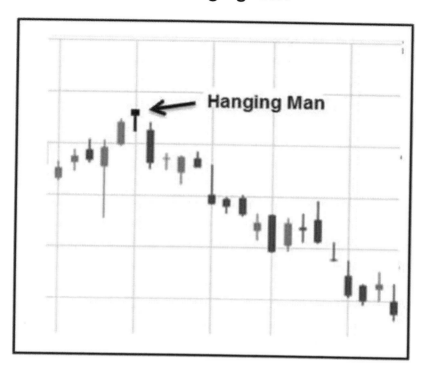

The **Hanging Man** is a bearish candlestick pattern that forms at the end of an uptrend. It looks like the Hammer, but it forms at the end of an advance instead of a decline like the Hammer. It is created when there is a significant sell-off near the market open, but buyers are able to push this stock back up to close at or near the opening price. Generally the large sell-off is seen as an early indication that the bulls (buyers) are losing control and demand for the asset is waning.

## The *Spinning Top*

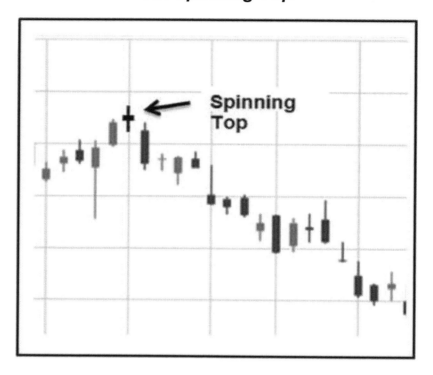

Spinning Top

The *Spinning Top* is a candlestick formation where the real body is small despite a wide range of price movement throughout the trading day. This candle is often regarded as neutral and used to signal indecision about the future direction of the stock's price. Most traders look at it as simply a ho-hum day and wait to see what the next day brings. The following day or two usually confirms if a reversal in trend is happening.

Confirmation the following day should indicate whether the advance will continue or a decline will ensue. In the above case, the confirmation was a negative candle the following day certainly indicating a change in trend.

# CHAPTER 5

## *Formations*

### *The TRI Star*

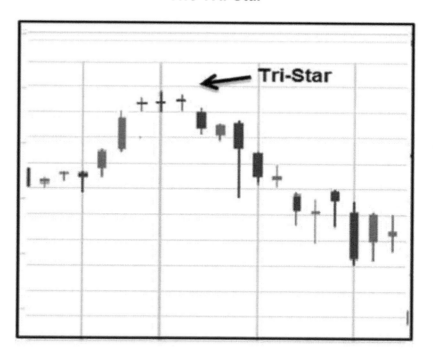

The ***Tri-Star*** is another type of candlestick pattern that signals a reversal in the current trend. This pattern is formed when three consecutive DOJI candlesticks appear after the stock has experienced an advance in price.

The above chart illustrates a bearish tri-star pattern at the top of the uptrend and is used to mark the beginning of a shift in momentum. A seasoned trader would be thinking, "Look out below!"

Keep in mind that even though the tri-star in this chart is clearly formed, many times there may only be 2 stars. Also note that these 'stars' are actually DOJI candles, signifying that neither the buyers nor the sellers have control since the stock opened and closed at virtually the same price on all three days. When you think about neither the buyers nor sellers having control and the DOJI forms at the end of an uptrend or a down-trend, then many times a change in direction is likely. In this case, three DOJIs formed. But the important thing is what had happened previously.

The point is a trend in a particular stock or the overall market takes time. We are always looking for recognizable candles, patterns, or formations to appear at the *end* of an advance or decline. I would prefer to see a stock advance or decline a minimum of five days and then see a bottom or top forming.

This lets us ignore small candles that appear a day or two after a change in trend has happened.

## *The Bearish Harami*

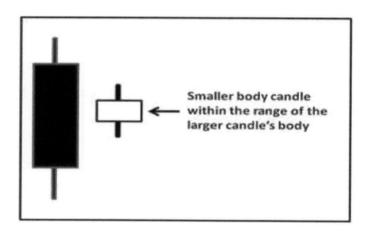

Smaller body candle within the range of the larger candle's body

The **Bearish Harami** is a pattern that forms at the top after an advance. It is indicated by a large *dark* candlestick that forms on a negative trading day signaling a change may be in store. Then it is followed by a much smaller candlestick with a body that is located within the vertical range of the larger candle's body. Such a pattern is an indication that the previous upward trend is coming to an end.

When you think about it, the lower close of the Bearish candle is an early warning sign. When this candle forms after an advance, you know the sellers have stepped in. Even before the next candle forms you should be on high alert if you are holding this stock. Then when the next candle is formed showing the price cannot penetrate the upper area of the previous candle, this sometimes indicates a top has been reached and often times reverse in direction will soon take place.

## *The Bullish Harami*

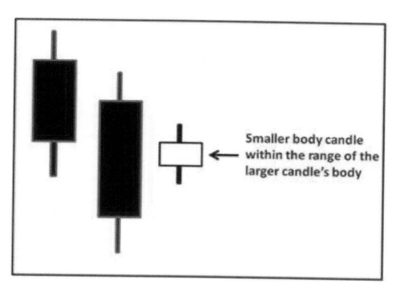

Smaller body candle within the range of the larger candle's body

The Bullish Harami pattern may look very close to the same as the Bearish Harami, but it forms at the bottom after a decline in the stock's price.

The **Bullish Harami** is a candlestick chart pattern in which a large candlestick is followed by a smaller candlestick whose body is located within the vertical range of the larger body candle on the previous day. In terms of candlestick colors, the bullish harami is a downtrend of negative-colored candlesticks engulfing a small positive (white) candlestick, giving a sign of a reversal of the downward trend.

## *The Harami Cross*

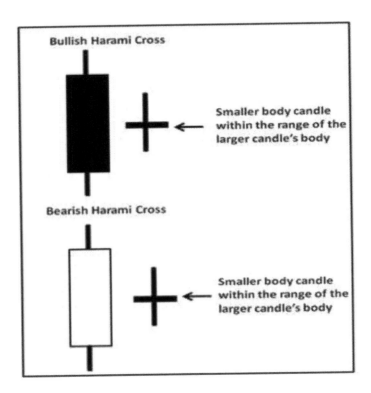

Bullish Harami Cross

Smaller body candle within the range of the larger candle's body

Bearish Harami Cross

Smaller body candle within the range of the larger candle's body

The *Harami Cross* is like the previous Harami formations except the small body candle is a DOJI. This indicates that the previous trend is about to reverse.

Think trader psychology for a moment. With the Bearish Harami Cross, what might have happened in the trading that formed this particular pattern?

Obviously the large white candle was formed with the market opening and the stock trading higher to the close that day. But on the following day, there are a couple of things we need to mention about the DOJI.

1) The stock could not trade above the previous day's range, and

2) No one had control. It was an even match between the buyers and the sellers.

Now, think about it a little further. If on this day when the DOJI is formed there are no longer enough buyers to push the price higher, and the sellers continue to sell at this price preventing an advance, the DOJI tells us that when the buyers and sellers are equal, then further advance may be unlikely.

The Bullish Harami is just opposite. There were not enough sellers to push the price lower, meaning, the buyers stepped in after a decline in price and began buying at that level. So once again, the DOJI tells the story and indicates a change in direction.

## The Bullish Engulfing Pattern

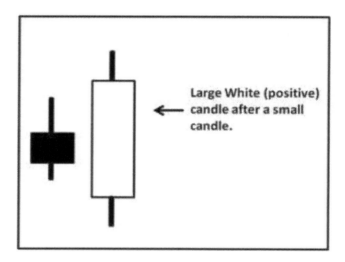

The **Bullish Engulfing Pattern** is a chart pattern that forms when a small black candlestick is followed by a large white candlestick that completely eclipses or "engulfs" the previous day's candlestick. The previous day's candle can be negative or positive, it really doesn't matter that much. What matters is the large positive candle is saying the selling may be over.

When this pattern forms after a downward trend, a trader sees this as a signal that the decline is ending and a reversal is about to take place.

Remember the DOJI? In this case, the small-bodied candle that formed at the bottom of the downtrend could also have been a DOJI. First signaling a reversal, and in the above picture the reversal came the following day with the bullish engulfing candle. That would be the confirmation of a change in direction.

## *The Bearish Engulfing Pattern*

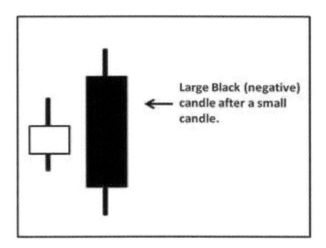

This is simply the opposite of the Bullish Engulfing pattern. It forms after an advancing trend and signals that a reversal is about to take place.

When you see the Bearish Engulfing pattern form after a stock has been trending up, then there is a pretty clear signal that change in direction is in the air.

Both the Bullish and Bearish Engulfing patterns are very telling indicators. After an advance in price, the Bearish Candle certainly signifies the sellers have stepped in. Conversely, after a decline, the Bullish Engulfing Candle tells us the buyers have started buying and further decline may not be likely.

## The RISING THREE METHODS

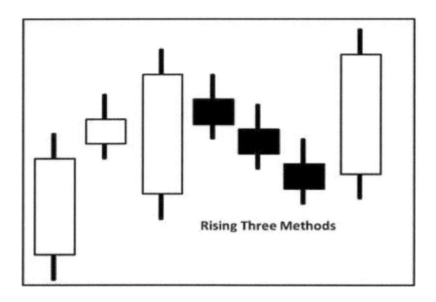

Rising Three Methods

The **Rising Three Methods** is a bullish candlestick pattern that is used to predict the continuation of the current uptrend. As you can see, the trend has been advancing but there are three negative days in a row. However, notice the trading range of the negative days never trades below the large positive candle to the left. This indicates the advance will likely continue. Another way to look at this formation is that the stock is taking a rest, or a breather, so to speak. Just a slight pullback before it marches higher.

## *The Falling Three Methods*

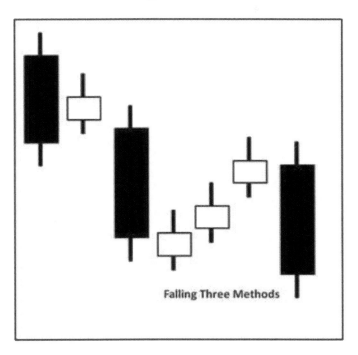

Falling Three Methods

The *Falling Three Methods* is pretty much the opposite of the Rising Three Methods. It's a bearish candlestick pattern that tells us the current downtrend will probably continue. As I said previously, stock prices never move in a straight line. In this case, if the primary trend is down, then any bounce in the stock price is usually going to be met with more selling.

I might add that during market declines, many traders look at little advances in price as an opportunity to short-sell the stock. And, sometimes the little advances are caused by the short-sellers buying to take their profits from the preceding decline.

## The Bearish Abandoned Baby

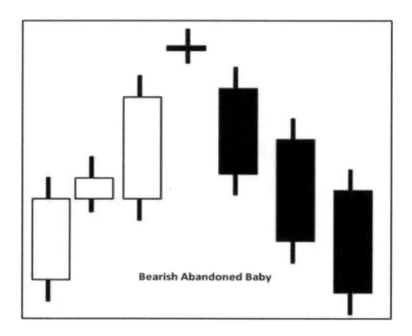

Bearish Abandoned Baby

The **Bearish Abandoned Baby** is a candlestick pattern that usually tells us a reversal in the current uptrend is on its way.

First of all, the previous advance is eclipsed by a DOJI. That in itself is our first signal, but the confirmation comes the next day with a bearish engulfing candle. When you look at an advance in a stock's price while viewing a chart and see the DOJI and then see heavy selling the following day that should be enough to get your attention.

If fact, experienced traders who see this pattern form and are holding the stock, usually begin to look back on a longer term chart to see where support might be found for the stock's price. If it is very far below the current price, they would exit the trade.

## The Bullish Abandoned Baby

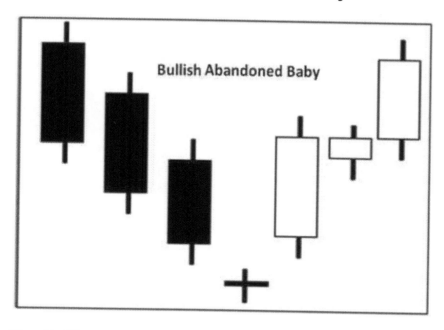

Bullish Abandoned Baby

The **Bullish Abandoned Baby** is the mirror image of the Bearish counterpart.

And once again, the DOJI is the first sign of change. It appears at the bottom, after a decline, telling us the buyers and sellers are virtually equal. The confirmation of this pattern is the positive candle the very next day.

# CHAPTER 6

## *More Formations*

### *Three Black Crows*

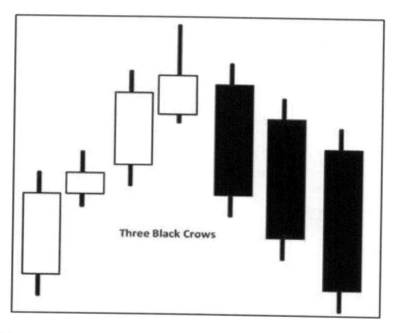

This pattern consists of three consecutive long-bodied, negative, candlesticks that have closed lower than the previous day with each session's open occurring within the body of the previous candle.

This is a scary sight if you are holding a stock and see this pattern form. Selling is heavy, and not for just one day. Further decline is almost certain.

There is normally some serious selling affiliated when the Crows are formed. Furthermore, a large bearish engulfing candle should always be of grave concern even if it is not associated with other similar candles such as in the formation above. One large black candle should be enough to get your full attention, especially after an uptrend.

## *Three White Soldiers*

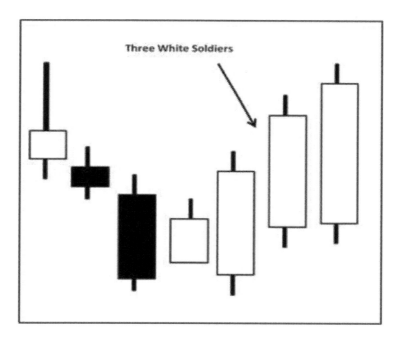

**The *Three White Soldiers*** is obviously a bullish candlestick pattern.

This pattern consists of three consecutive long-bodied positive candlesticks that have closed higher than the previous day, with each session's open occurring within the body of the previous candle.

Let's take another look at this chart for an important lesson.

Yes, you can easily see the Three White Soldiers. But what else can you see?

Notice the bottom candle on the chart is a large bearish engulfing candle, but the following day there is a white candle. This is the white candle to right side of the lowest engulfing candle.

There are several things to learn here.

1) It is very close to the Bullish Harami discussed earlier.
2) After the price closed at the bottom of the negative candle, the price 'Gapped' up the following day to open for trading higher than it closed the previous day.
3) It NEVER traded lower than it opened. We know this because there is no WICK on the lower end of that candle. So this would be our first signal that a reversal was about to happen.
4) Then of course the huge engulfing candle the following day would serve as additional

confirmation if the Trader wanted to wait for it to form.

One Trading strategy here would have been to buy on the first confirmation, and place a stop loss below the area believed to be support. This would be a very low risk trade with the opportunity for a sizable gain. At this point, if the stock had been in a decline for awhile, we would be anticipating a bottom at some point. So, after the positive candle formed with no wick on the bottom of it, we could believe that a support level had been reached at that price. Then the following day, the stock traded higher. So this would provide the opportunity to enter the trade at a low risk and place a stop loss just below the support level. This protects the investment capital from significant loss, and, provides the opportunity for a sizable gain.

This is a great example of *Risk versus Reward*. The stock has been in a downtrend and then appears to have found support. This is where a Stop Loss is your insurance against significant loss and allows you to enter a position while limiting your possible loss.

Now let's look at some of these different candles and formations in real application.

Notice on the chart below how the stock has traded in a downtrend from the upper left of the chart for about 14 days from the high of around $120. (Count the candles from the beginning of the decline. Each candle represents one trading day.) The price continues each day trading lower toward the $100 area.

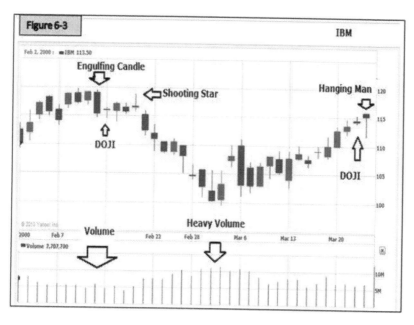

As the stock trades lower each day, *what* is the volume doing?

Right! It is increasing. The volume is *confirming the trend.* We always check the volume. If a stock is advancing and the volume is declining, then it is not confirming the trend. Notice as this stock reached the bottom and closed at the $100 range on one day, then opened slightly higher the next day, and moved up to close higher that day on heavy volume. This forms the Bullish Engulfing Candle at the bottom.

## What does this tell you?

**Remember:** The Stock Market is a ZERO SUM game. For every Seller there is a Buyer, and vice versa.

This chart shows a perfect example of the 'Bulls and the Bears' slugging it out as the stock moved down. Selling pressure increased as shown in the volume. Support was finally found and the Bulls won. Meaning simply at the $100 range, there were more buyers than there were sellers. Supply and demand at its finest, all of that information right there on a simple chart.

## What else does this chart tell you?

One thing in particular is: How many warnings does a trader need? On the left side of the chart when the stock topped out at $120, there are at least three warnings that the advance was ending and a change in direction was coming. If the first Bearish Engulfing candle wasn't enough of a warning, there was a DOJI and a Shooting Star to follow. Not to mention a candle very close to the appearance of a Hanging Man and another Spinning Top. All of those candles were within the body of the large engulfing candle.

If you were thinking of trading or investing in this stock at some time in the future, you would pull up a chart on this stock and would easily see that back on this particular occasion there was 'Support' for this stock at the $100 range. Knowing this, you could make an informed trading or investing decision based on what the stock was selling for at the time. You would know if you purchased this stock at, let's say, $105, then it should not fall more than $5 before it found support.

## What else does this chart tell you?

You would know that *if* you had purchased this stock at $105 sometime in the future, and it fell through the support level of $100 then there must be a reason for this and you might want to close your position to prevent further loss. You don't wait to see if it will trade back above support, remember: "When in doubt, get out."

## What else does this chart tell you?

Look at the highs of around $120 reached by this stock shown on the chart in the upper left area.

Now look at what the stock is doing as it moves up to the right side of the chart.

Look, in particular, the vertical bars get shorter just like they did on the left side when the stock moved up toward the $120 range. This tells you the 'Trading Range' each day is closing in, there's less volatility, and it's becoming more difficult to advance.

## *What does that mean?*

Supply and demand. The number of buyers and the number of sellers are becoming equal. Also note the volume. As the stock trades higher, the volume decreases. The volume is not confirming the trend. When you think 'Trader Psychology,' it indicates there are fewer buyers as the price advances, and that the number of buyers and sellers are becoming equal.

And another thought: Who would be the likely sellers and who would be the buyers as the price advanced? Would a professional looking at a chart of this stock be jumping on the bandwagon and buying shares as the stock nears the $120 range? No, not very likely. The buyers are more likely the novices.

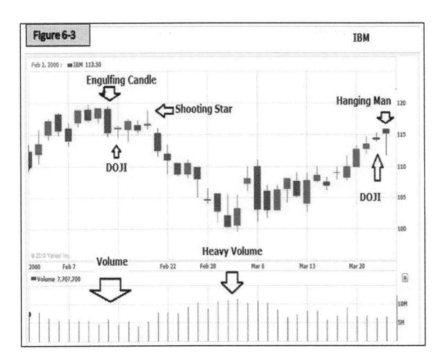

Figure 6-3                                    IBM

## What else can we learn from this chart?

Notice the last bar on the right side of the chart.

That day the stock opened and closed at practically the same price and formed a Hanging Man candle.

VERY IMPORTANT: Anytime a stock has had a significant move either up OR down over a period of several days or weeks, and you see a daily bar like that one, it indicates the stock is likely going to move in the opposite direction over the next few days.

The day before was a **"Spinning Top,"** an early warning of a change in direction.

## *What else do you see on this Chart?*

Just as important as other points made, on the right side of the chart, the stock is once again reaching the $120 range. This is where it was on the left side of the chart when it dropped over the course of about 14 days to find support.

RESISTANCE: Yes, the $120 price range is upper resistance for this stock. It could not penetrate the $120 range in February on the left side of the chart and here it is 30 days later reaching that level again.

What if you were going to trade or invest in this stock?

## For instance:

1) If you were going to trade this stock, or even invest for the long term, why would you be buying it at the $118 to $120 range? You wouldn't! But remember the Stock Market is a zero sum game. Someone bought that stock at $120, and someone sold it!

2) Who are the likely 'Sellers' at the $120 range and who are the likely 'Buyers' at the $120 range? The Pros are the ones that **were buying** it at the support level around $100 and those buyers are now the Sellers at $120.

The buyers at $120 are obviously inexperienced and uninformed and have no training on chart analysis. They are jumping in *hoping* the stock will continue to advance.

One more thing about the volume:

When the stock sold off for 14 days and then found support. The volume increased. Now think trading psychology again. The buyers up at the $120 range are obviously giving up, afraid of further loses, and the Pros have been sitting idly by waiting for the stock to reach support. When support is reached, they step in. So you have the informed buyers moving back in to the stock and the uninformed sellers throwing in the towel at the same time, thus, the increased volume, and no further decline.

This is also a good lesson in patience. A new investor or trader usually lacks patience and has the tendency to want to jump in, fearful of missing out on an advance. Don't make that mistake. Wait for the confirmation. Buy at the bottom, not at the top. And, always use a Stop Loss to protect your capital.

*"Nothing gives one person so much advantage over another as to remain cool and unruffled under all circumstances"*

*~Thomas Jefferson*

# CHAPTER 7

## *Support, Resistance, and Trends*

With what we have covered so far, let's look a little closer at Support - Resistance, and Trends. Also note on the Chart below I am introducing you to "Gaps." A price Gap is when the opening price for the day is higher than the previous day closing price, thus causing a gap in pricing. A gap shows up on the chart as a space between the trading range from one day to the next.

You should understand the importance of support and resistance. The more you watch the market and individual stocks, the more you will come to appreciate its significance.

The following chart shows as the stock advanced from the left side of the chart, it hit resistance at about the $31.00 price range. Then as it declined, it found support at $24.00. And then, as it advanced once again it 'bumped its head' on resistance before falling back to support once again.  See Figure 8-1 below.

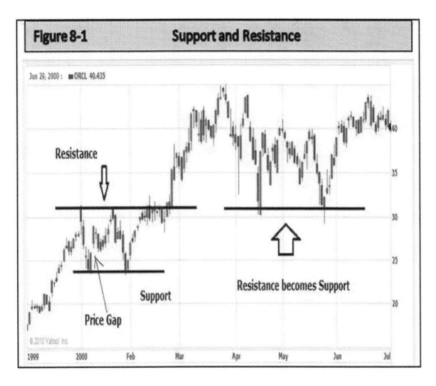

**Figure 8-1**    **Support and Resistance**

First of all, look at the first resistance level shown on the above chart at around $31. See what happened when this stock hit that resistance? It pulled back to find support at $24. It then advanced to hit resistance again, and then fell back to support.

But after hitting the support the second time, it moved through the resistance to trade higher.

This is what is called a 'Break Out,' where the stock breaks out above a prior resistance level.

## *What does this tell us?*

First of all, once breaking through resistance, then that prior resistance becomes support. Secondly, after breaking out above the first resistance level, we now know that this stock has two support levels. One around $31, the previous resistance, and if it fell through that one, it may find support again around $24, the old support level.

This clearly shows how powerful a support level can be. After breaking through resistance, the stock later fell back to the new support level two times, and did not fall through.

What else?

Applying what you have learned so far, if you were going to purchase this stock, where would be a good entry point?

When the stock traded down to support the second time? Yes. It is very common for a stock to *test* a support level, which this one clearly did. This forms a chart pattern known as a Double Bottom.

So, yes, purchasing it in the $25 to $26 range would be a good move, and you would know there was support immediately below that level. So, given a worst case scenario, and the stock turned and started falling, you would be able to close the position (sell) for only a small loss if it fell through the support level. A great place to have a Stop Loss for your trade would be just under the support level. Typically, a stop loss should be a few cents lower than known support, and in this case, the stop loss would have been at about $23.50, fifty cents below the $24 known support level.

Where would be another *entry point* to purchase?

After it broke through resistance at $31. Knowing that there was resistance at that level, unless you purchased close to the old support level of $24 you wouldn't be buying as it approached resistance again. Just like we learned studying the earlier chart, if you are going to be an active participant, trading this stock, you don't want to be the buyer when the stock is approaching a known resistance level. You would either be the seller, or you would be tightening up your Stop Loss levels to preserve gains.

In this scenario, if you had purchased the stock while it was close to the previous support and now it is trading up close to resistance, what do you do?

By purchasing around $25, you actually now have the luxury of being in a profitable position, so you have several options available:

1) You could simply sell out with a profit. But you would probably want to consider 'Market Strength' and other factors we will cover later before simply clicking the 'Sell' button.

2) You could place a Stop Loss order below the current price as *insurance* in case the stock price dropped, you would be sold out and your profit would be protected. (We will also cover Stop Loss orders later)

3) You might simply make a 'Mental Note' (although mental notes are not recommended) as to where you would sell in case the price started falling so you would protect your profit, and then continue to hold the position (stock) in case of a breakout to the upside which would be even more profitable for you.

**NOTE:** One final thing about the previous chart before we move on:

I want to mention this now even though we will cover it later. Notice the price GAP, indicated by the arrow, the stock made when it moved off the first support and headed up to the resistance level. You see where it closed one day around $26, and then opened the next day around $27 causing the price gap? This gap shows up on the chart as an open space separating the daily candles. This is very important. To keep it simple for now, I'll just say that GAPS historically are filled, or closed. Meaning at some point in time, the stock price will fall back to that area, or trade lower, to close that gap. If you look ahead on the chart you will see what happened.

Yes, over the next month, the stock fell back and closed that gap. Gaps are not always closed – but the market does not like Gaps, and Gaps are historically closed, more often than not.

Let's look at that chart once again. We see the *role reversal* of a breakout above $31. This is a classic example of breaking through resistance and then the prior resistance becoming support in the future. See Figure 8-1 below.

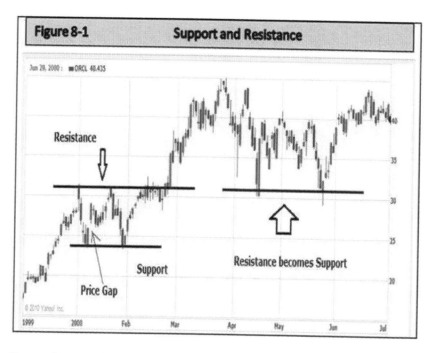

See how the stock advanced after breaking the resistance at $31 and then declined to find support at the old resistance level. This is very common.

Let's talk a bit more about Gaps.

Look at the very first gap on this chart shown toward the lower left corner. Notice how the stock advanced toward its first high creating gaps at the $24 and the $29 range, and then over the course of about a week traded lower to close those gaps.

It is important to note that the gap created during the first advance at the $24 range was closed, but that range also became support. This is also very common.

To help you understand the reasoning behind a Gap becoming a support level, think of it this way. Let's say a stock was finding resistance at $87 per share because that was about the maximum the company was worth at the time. Remember, the market discounts everything, past, present, and future.

But if the company announced positive earnings, introduced a new product on the market, or something significant that either causes the company to be worth more money or possibly have a better outlook for increased earnings in the future, then suddenly the price may increase. This increase would be justified by the new information or product. Suddenly the stock price jumps as the market is factoring in or discounting the new information, and it gaps open the next trading day to $90 per share. With the new information discounted into the price, now a price below $87 would be undervalued because of the new information, earnings outlook, whatever. Since the market discounts everything, the new perceived value has increased. So if the price drops to $87 or below, investors realize this is a bargain and start buying, which in turn, increases the price, thus forming the support level at the old Gap in price.

Many factors are possibly responsible for the type of stock movement in the previous chart where it makes a strong move over a short period gapping up three times in rapid succession. You will likely never know what the underlying reason is for a pullback or an advance in a stock's price. But the information you are learning here gives you the tools to better protect you from losses and capitalize on profits to be made.

Entry and exit points are vital parts of trading and investing. That is worth repeating.

## Entry and Exit points are vital parts of Trading and Investing.

Whether you are Day Trading, Swing Trading, or are a Long Term Investor. Why would you *ever* buy a stock at the *wrong* time? Unfortunately, there are many market participants with no training that do it every day.

The Pros love the uninformed, the novices, and the Pigs. Who else are they going to sell to when a stock has reached a resistance point, or reached an all time high?

You guessed it. They are going to sell to the novices and the pigs who are hoping for more advance. Then when the stock drops, falls to support, or finds support somewhere, the Pros will buy it back from the novice who has just taken a loss and a beating.

*"The time to buy is when blood is running in the streets" ~Baron Rothschild*

# CHAPTER 8

## *Trend Lines*

Earlier we learned about support, resistance, gaps, entry, and exit points. We will now build on that information and at times, refer back to those items. Let's look at a trend line.

In the following chart we see a trend line drawn connecting the support levels where the stock has found support on 3 separate occasions. See Figure 9-1 below.

Figure 9-1   Rising Trend Line

Uptrend Drawn under rising lows

It only takes two points, or lows, to draw a trend line. Meaning, the trend line drawn in the above chart could have effectively been drawn after the stock had found support at point 1 and at point 2. However, while it only takes two points to draw a trend line, a third point is necessary to identify the line as a valid trend line.

## *How does this help us?*

By drawing a trend line connecting points 1 and 2, we can then extend the trend line to the 'infinite.' Understand?

As we learned from the Dow Theory, once a trend is started it continues. Yes, it does until something happens and causes the stock to change its direction and start a new trend.

So by looking at the above chart we see that the trend line starting at support point 1, and extended past (support) point 2 gives us a good idea as to where the stock might find support during any pullbacks in price. And as the chart clearly shows, that is what happened when the stock eventually traded higher and pulled back to find support right along the trend line.

The idea here, as you can see, is that this trend line is extended and continues to follow the stock.

This trend line creates buy (entry) points to purchase the stock. This is a great tool to use when considering trading or investing in a stock and looking for a place to enter. An advancing stock will pull back and usually find support very close to the trend line. That becomes a good entry point for a couple of reasons.

1) The trend line itself serves are minor support.
2) The stock has pulled back from a high and as it reaches the trend line, it is normally not that far from the previous low. This allows you to enter a position and place a stop loss just under the previous low. This limits any possible loss in case the stock turns and trades lower instead of advancing as you anticipate.

What we have just learned is drawing a trend line connecting the Lows/Support, and how to interpret it.

Remember: As a rule, the longer a trend line has been in effect and the more times it has been tested, the more significant it becomes. The violation of a trend line is often the best warning of a change in trend. In other words, if the stock falls through the trend line, you should pay attention, it is important.

This can be an invaluable tool for the long-term investor. The Primary Trend of the market can be easily tracked along with the trend of any particular investments.

Thus, the astute investor would be warned if the general market trend changed. Thus, a re-balance of the portfolio might be in order. Possibly even sell some holdings to prevent losses and lock in the gains.

Since we know that once a trend is established, the general movement continues in the direction of that trend, it makes little sense to continue to hold on to mounting losses once a trend has been broken.

I use a long-term investor in this explanation because many traders are quick to exit a position. But long-term investors are more apt to hold on. Problem is, one never knows where the bottom is. It could be a 50% or 60% loss or even more. So it is always better to be safe than sorry. Lock in the gains and watch for a support level to be reached.

A trend line also gives us a great idea as to where a stock should fall to, or pullback to, when looking to buy. In the above chart, if you were looking to invest in that stock, you could simply draw a trend line and wait for the stock price to pull back to the trend line to buy. That way you would not be buying after an advance and then suffer the loss during a pullback. Instead, you would be buying at the 'low.'

**Channel Lines**

Channel lines are straight lines that are drawn parallel to basic trend lines. A rising channel line would be drawn above the price action and parallel to the basic trend line (which is below the price action) connecting the "highs" that the stock has reached.

In the following chart you can see a channel line drawn connecting the highs and is parallel to the trend line drawn below connecting the lows. See Figure 9-2 below.

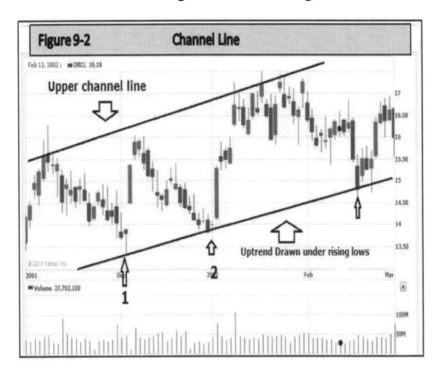

Overall markets and stocks often trend within a channel. When this is the case, the chartist can use that knowledge to great advantage by knowing in advance where support and resistance are likely to be found.

As a trader, what if you purchased this stock as it found support the second time? You could then draw the trend and channel lines. Once it advanced to the upper channel line, you would know it may be time for a pullback. You could take your profit and wait for another opportunity to enter at a lower price.

You can see that the channel line tells us where the next 'higher high' should be found before the stock trades up to it.

The above stock traded in a channel during the decline. By drawing the trend and channel lines, one would know where the stock price was likely headed if it continued to decline. You would also be alerted when it broke out of the channel, as it did on the right side of the chart after finding support. At that point, a new trend began.

## So how does this help us?

Again, this is all about entry and exit points. A short-term trader can take advantage of this information to exit at the highs and re-enter at the lows. A Day Trader might even exit a long position (sell) at the high and then go short (sell short) at the high to grab a quick profit on the pullback. Although 'Shorting' a strong stock in an uptrend would certainly not be advisable, but shorting a stock in a downtrend when it reaches the highs of a downward sloping channel line can be a very good entry point for a short sale.

A long term investor can use this information to help find good entry points as well. Following a trend can alert the investor that the stock has reached support and it is time to buy. Trends also help prevent buying at the wrong time. For instance, the more cautious investor may wait until the stock has broken out of the upper channel line during a move to the upside. This would be another confirmation that support had truly been found and the trend had changed.

In the above chart – imagine a long-term investor had drawn a trend line on the previous advance (not shown), sold when the old trend line was broken around $150 per share, and then waited for support and a new entry point. He would have re-entered around the $130 per share area, thus avoiding a $20 per share decline in his investing account.

You might think in this instance that saving $20 per share is insignificant and possibly not worth the trouble. However, as this chart was forming and the old trend line was broken, there was no way of knowing that support would be found or held at the $130 range. To exit when the trend was broken is moving to safety to prevent significant loss. Meaning, the stock could have continued to fall, taking your dollars with it. As an example, see Figure 9-4 below.

**IMPORTANT**: Any trader or investor can use this information as a valuable tool.

For instance: A long-term investor holding a stock sees that the stock has broken a trend line and closed lower.

This information can, and should be used as an *alert* that the trend may be changing.

The above chart shows how a trend can be broken. Once a trend is broken, a new trend begins. In the above case it appears obvious the new trend is to the downside.

Even if this investor has already held this stock for a long period of time, why allow a profit to turn into a loss? When the above stock broke the trend line at $9.50 per share, there is no way of knowing, and certainly no guarantee that support will be found, ever. This information is highly valuable in the decision making process. The long-term investor sees a potential problem, and sets an *alert*, or a Stop Loss. Thus protecting any accumulated profit and preventing any loss.

On the other hand, a trader, or short-term investor, sees the same decline and makes decisions accordingly; possibly even shorting the stock at the high before the decline started or once the trend has been broken. In the above case, a trader using a trend line would recognize the stock fell through the trend line and then traded back up but could not make a higher high, or even close above the old trend. In other words, that would be a great shorting opportunity, *selling the first lower high*.

In looking at the above chart – notice after the trend line was broken, then the stock sold off creating the two big engulfing candles, and then it *gapped* down. This is pretty classic. What typically happens is this: After the first big down candle, the traders start jumping in selling short.

The increased selling pressure causes the significant move to the downside. As you can see, about a week later the gap was almost closed.

But the main point here is, once that first engulfing candle formed after the trend was broken, that was confirmation for many that the stock was headed lower. So they start selling short and the stock falls. That is why it is always important to take action early. Taking action early can prevent getting caught in a sell off and watching your money vanish into thin air. This is also when trading and investing strategies are of upmost importance.

For instance:

A long-term investor might continue to hold the stock for whatever reason, possibly tax reasons, but he or she could purchase a *PUT* Option on the stock at the current price to protect the profit, and/or gain that has been accumulated since entering the position.

Thus, if the price continues to decline, the value of the Put Option increases, therefore offsetting some of the loss incurred by the falling stock price.

If the stock price turns and continues to advance, then the Put Option can be sold at a reduced price and the small loss on the Option would be simply "Insurance" paid for protection. Protecting one's capital is always most important.

Another alternative:

If you were a long-term holder of this stock and believed that it might continue to decline before finding support, you could sell a Covered-Call Option at, or just above, the current price. This way you receive the premium from the option buyer, and if the price does not increase above the option strike price prior to its expiration, then the option expires worthless. But you still keep the premium you collected on the option, and possibly even sell another one. This premium paid to you for the option is profit that can offset the loss in the stock price.

The point is, sitting idly by watching your money vanish as a stock declines can be financial suicide. You must have a plan to protect your capital. Either sell the stock to prevent loss, buy put options, or sell covered calls. Do something! Money is too hard to come by to simply stick your head in the sand and let it disappear. It is far easier to *keep* your money, than to have to try to make again.

# CHAPTER 9

## *Chart Patterns*

One of the more useful features of chart analysis is the presence of price patterns, which can be classified into different categories and most can have very predictive value.

These patterns reveal the ongoing struggle between the forces of supply and demand, as seen in the relationship between the various support and resistance levels, and allow the chartist to gauge which side is winning. Then, it's only a matter of understanding and interpreting the information correctly.

Price patterns are broken down into two groups—reversal and continuation patterns.

*Reversal* patterns usually indicate that a trend reversal is taking place. These patterns are your early warning signs if you are holding the stock and are your alerts if you are considering buying it. These patterns are also very predictable once they have formed.

*Continuation* patterns usually represent temporary pauses in the existing trend.

Continuation patterns take less time to form than reversal patterns and usually result in resumption of the original trend.

There are numerous patterns that we will cover. Chart patterns are called 'Patterns' for a reason. It is because they historically have proven to be indicators and great tools as to what is about to happen in the future with a stock price and/or the market as a whole.

These distinctive 'Patterns' are formed by the price action of a stock, and through the years the patterns have been named, most often in relation to what they resemble when looking at them on a chart.

With just a little time, you should be able to recognize them quickly to be warned when one of your stocks is about to decline or alerted when a buying opportunity is about to happen.

We will first look at reversal patterns. Reversal patterns are highly important for finding entry and exit points, setting alerts, and warning the investor of possible declines.

# Reversal Patterns

## "The Head and Shoulders"

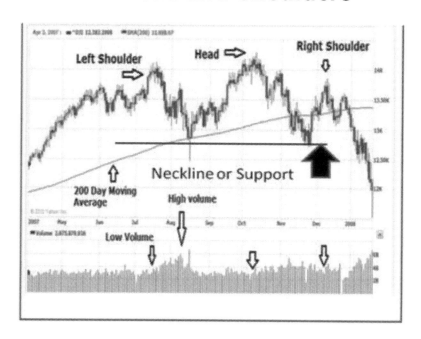

The **Head and Shoulders** is one of the best known and probably the most reliable of the reversal patterns. A head and shoulders top is characterized by three prominent market peaks.

While the peak, or the *head*, is higher than the two surrounding peaks (*the shoulders*), as this pattern was forming, your original trend and/or channel line would have been headed upward and would have been on the low after the first shoulder was formed. That trend line would have been broken after the head was formed and the ensuing low was reached. A new trend line would have had be drawn that now is actually *the neckline*, which is drawn below the two intervening reaction lows. Remember, the preceding upward trend was already broken when the second low was reached, and now a close below the neckline completes the pattern and signals an important market reversal. Let's take a look at a *Head and Shoulders* reversal that started a Bear Market which led to a severe market decline. See Figure 10-3 below.

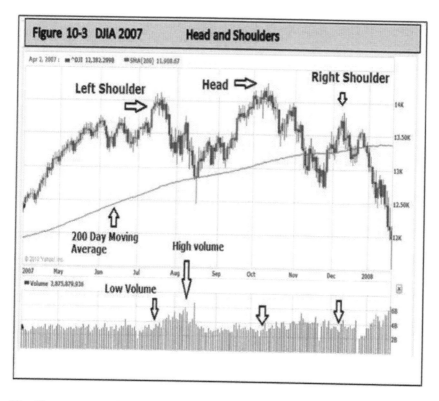

**By the way... Does the above chart look familiar?**

Yes, this is a chart of the Dow Jones Industrial Average during the all-time-high set in October of 2007. And as you remember – that was the beginning of a major bear market.

First of all - Look at the clear Head and Shoulders Pattern. The left shoulder was the first high. Then the head is the all-time-high. Then the right shoulder is the third high, also called the third 'Peak.'

### This is a classic 'Head and Shoulders' Pattern.

When you see one of these forming whether it is on an individual stock, index fund, or in this case, the Dow Jones Industrial Average, it is time to 'Sit up and Pay Attention!'

This formation is one of the most reliable chart patterns you will see. Remember the 'Distribution Phase' of market cycles from chapter one? This is it. Obviously, the distribution phase was underway after the first shoulder was formed.

How do we know that Distribution was underway after the first peak? Volume. The heavy volume during the pullback after the high on the left shoulder is our first clue. Look at the increased volume during that pullback. It tells us there was heavy selling, and, it tells us the volume was not confirming the uptrend that had been in place. In order for volume to confirm the uptrend, you want to see higher volume during advances and lower volume during pullbacks.

Let's take a closer look at the volume, and how volume must confirm the trend.
See Figure 10-3 below.

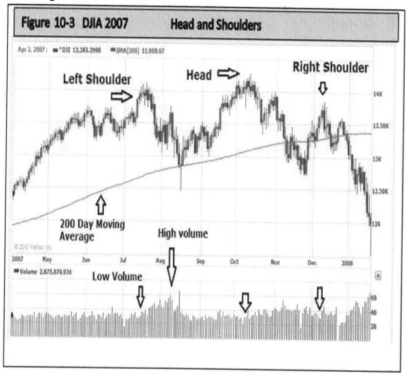

Figure 10-3  DJIA 2007          Head and Shoulders

When looking at the volume across the bottom of the chart, as the first high formed (Left Shoulder), volume was a little higher. Normally that is good. It is nice to see a stock, or in this case the market, make a higher high on increased volume. But during the sell-off after the first high, the volume was higher than the volume of the advance while making the high. Thus, *distribution*...

Now notice the volume on the all-time-high (Head) is decreased volume. This is *more* distribution. The volume is not confirming the trend. The volume then increases on the next pullback. Inexperienced buyers are scooping up the stock and the Pros are happy to sell. Make no mistake, distribution is always a result of the Pros selling (distributing) their shares to the uninformed, the novices, the unsuspecting, and yes, the pigs that are greedy and hoping for more of an advance.

Now look at the volume on the third high (Right Shoulder). Yep, we're in trouble now! The pullbacks and sell-offs after each high were on increased volume. Thus, more and more distribution, and more lambs being led to the slaughter. More dumb money listening to TV Talking Heads claiming all sorts of brainless prophecies.

At this point the market is still trading above support levels. No major concerns, right?

At about this time you probably became dreadfully tired of the 'Talking Heads' on every financial news network proclaiming all sorts of things. Personally, I remember hearing some who claimed that the DOW could, and should, reach 20,000. Do you think the ones claiming this had just purchased stocks 'hoping' for farther advance in the market? Maybe... Or they may be selling and want to keep the buyers coming so they can unload.

Let's also apply a little common sense. When the high at the first shoulder is reached, the DJIA is about 1000 points above the 200-day moving average. Once again, when the head (all-time high) is formed the DJIA is about 1000 points above the 200-day moving average. Who sees this and realizes at the very least there is most likely going to be a pullback or correction and begins selling? Yes, the smart money, the experienced traders. Sure, some might not sell out completely, but will certainly cut back and/or go to cash to preserve most of their profits. At the very minimum, tightening up the stop loss would be the smart thing to do. Simply, a stock, or the market, will normally not trade too far above the 200 Day Moving Average for a long period of time before declining back closer to the moving average. In this instance, the market is 1000 points above the moving average, so a decline should be expected.

Now think *risk vs. reward*. Would a seasoned investor be buying a top? Would a smart investor be chasing the market, realizing there has been a long-term advance, buying in and hoping it will go higher? No! The risk of a correction is too high, and, the chance the market is going very much higher is very low.

As a chartist you can apply this knowledge to every investing and trading decision you make. For instance, before entering the market, you have to ask yourself:

1) What is the market currently doing?
2) Where is the market in relation to the moving averages?
3) What does the volume tell you?
4) What is the risk/reward?

5) Are you buying a bottom or are you chasing the market?
6) How do you protect your investment capital?

Every time you purchase an investment, your money is at risk. Therefore you must always make sure you are purchasing at a time when the risk is low, the reward is high, and your money is protected.

Let's look at support levels. Support levels are very important. We always want to know where support may be in case of a decline.

(See Figure 10-3 below)

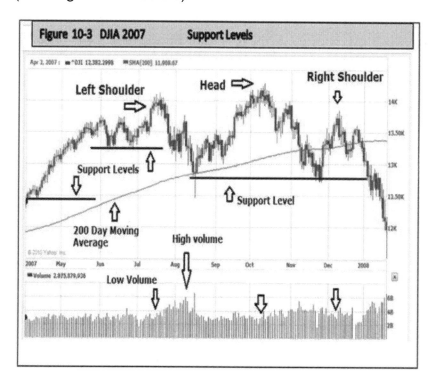

We see that there were only two support levels of any significance during this distribution phase. One was minor support just prior to the left shoulder and then there is the more significant support where the pullback landed on the 200-day moving average. The next significant support is found after the all-time high. These two significant support levels are what is considered the 'neckline' on this pattern.

The decline following the left shoulder top took about 30 days to find support and move higher to eventually form the highest peak, the head. That support level was tested and held prior to the right shoulder formation. But once that second support level was broken, a dramatic decline ensued. This is because the break below the neckline is confirmation of the head and shoulders pattern.

Note again, the volume increased as the market moved past the all-time-high and then past the right shoulder. See the increase in volume on the declines compared to the volume leading up to the highs? What does that tell you?

For one, increased volume certainly tells us that more stocks are changing hands, more buyers, more sellers, but the increase volume is happening during declines. The volume must confirm the trend. And in this case, the highs are on low volume and the sell-offs are on high volume. Thus indicating further advance is not likely, and, the volume is confirming the developing trend, a new downward trend.

I go into more depth about recognizing market tops and bottoms in my book, '*Trading the Trends*,' but this is classic for market tops. Historically, every market top has experienced the very same signals, warnings, and told the investors what it was about to do. There is always low volume on advances, higher volume on declines, along with trend lines and support broken. This scenario always leads to a new trend with lower highs and then lower lows. The right shoulder in this pattern is the first 'lower high.'

Let's look at one more thing using the very same chart. This time I added a trend line.

See Figure 10-4 below.

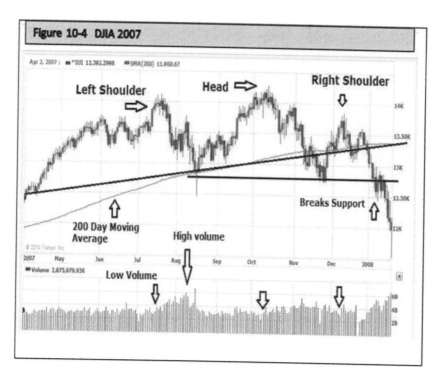

Figure 10-4  DJIA 2007

As we learned earlier, by connecting two or more lows, we can draw a trend line. The 200-day moving average is a trend line that can be added to any chart, and it is about as good as it gets, so to speak. The 200 DMA is also shown on the above chart.

Now take note of the volume when the market broke below the support line. Yes it was *increased volume*. Once the market closed below the support, **panic** ensued. Short Sellers piled on.

Yes, a dramatic decline hit. But that can be expected once support is broken. When you think about every decline during the distribution phase for the 6-months prior to breaking support, yes, the Pros were selling continually. Not so much to cause panic, but very methodically, and constantly selling. That is why the volume is low on advances when the market is topping out. The big money is not buying, they are gradually unloading. They wait for a little bounce and then sell into the strength. They are taking their profits. Many have been holding the stocks since they purchased them at the bottom during the previous 'Accumulation Phase.' In this case, that may have been in 2003 after the previous bear market when the internet bubble burst.

You see, the smart money knows that the market doesn't always go up. Anytime the DJIA is 1000 points above the 200-day moving average, the smart money expects a pullback. There is never any guarantee that a pullback will be just a small correction. Any pullback may turn into a major correction or a bear market with a thirty to fifty percent drop. Experienced traders take some money off the table at the tops. There is no sense in allowing a profit to disappear, or worse, turn into a loss.

Also note that after the all-time high was reached and the head of the pattern was formed, over the ensuing 45 days there were at least four big down days where the sell-off created dark engulfing candles. These are very telling! They are your early warning signs. They indicate what is to come.

## Moving Average

Moving averages are a very useful tool for determining trend. They can be applied to any chart. When displaying a chart, most will allow you to choose a 10-day moving average, a 20, 50, 100, or a 200-day moving average. The 200-day moving average is the most powerful of all. Whether you are dealing with an individual stock or a market index, when buying, your investment should be above the 200-day moving average (200 DMA). This average historically acts as both support and resistance. Meaning, if the stock or index is above the average, there should be support at or near the 200 DMA. If the stock or index falls below it, then the 200 DMA will usually act as resistance when the stock is trying to advance.

Notice in the above chart, in July, 2007 the first shoulder (peak) was formed, and then the market retreated to support right on the 200 DMA. Then after hitting the all-time-high, it fell through the 200 DMA.

Something significant – Take a look at the candle that formed when reaching the 200 DMA the second time. Do you see how it fell below the 200 DMA then traded higher to close above it? Yes, the following candle was a bearish engulfing candle that clearly fell through support of the 200 DMA. But think of the psychology of the traders and investors. Many obviously believed there would be support at the 200 DMA and started buying. This buying provided the close above the average. The support of the 200 DMA didn't last, but traders were obviously buying in hopes the support would hold.

The 200 DMA is historically a great tool for the long-term investor. It can be used to signal buy and sell points. Meaning, the investor simply sells out when the security falls below the 200 DMA and waits for the security to cross back above the 200 DMA to reenter the position.

## In Summary

Any way you look at the above charts of the Head and Shoulders formation – Any way you analyze it – even *pretend* that 2008 has not arrived yet, and you are looking at these charts as they form on a daily or weekly basis.

Whether you would have drawn a trend line on the lows leading up to the very first peak (left shoulder), or drawn a support line, or drawn a channel line, used a 100 DMA or a 200 DMA, the *result* would have been the same.

Once the market broke below the first line of support, and then broke the second line of support (neck line), the Head and Shoulders Pattern was formed.

Point is: By using Charting and Technical Analysis, you would have been *warned* and could have made adjustments in your portfolio, your holdings, and/or your trading strategies to protect your investment capital, and/or profits.

Remember: Investment firms and advisors do not want you to sell. They don't have a plan to protect your capital from losses, so it is always your responsibility to initiate changes to avoid loss of capital. Otherwise, you will find yourself holding a huge loss and hoping the market will come back so you can just break even.

Holding losses and hoping to break even is *not* an investing or trading plan. That is dumb money on suicide watch!

One more thing – then I'll move on. You may think that looking at a chart from 2007 – 2008 is insignificant, maybe even out-dated. You are wrong. This same pattern will form again, again, and again. You will see this pattern and all of the same breakdowns, the volume decrease on advances, the volume increase on declines, etc, over and over again.

These are tools to learn and to know that they will be just as relevant 10, 20, or 30 years from now. Never think that the market is 'different' today, or will be different tomorrow. It won't be…

Jesse Livermore said, "Nothing ever changes."

And it really doesn't. The market will make another high, there will be another bear market, investors will lose their capital, and the greedy and uninformed will buy the market tops.

Next time will not be different… It never has been different and very will be.

Let's look at an inverted head and shoulders pattern.

# CHAPTER 10

## *Inverted Head and Shoulders Pattern*

The inverted head and shoulders pattern is the mirror image of the head and shoulders we just discussed.

This is also a very powerful pattern that every trader and investor should easily recognize. Notice the right shoulder is not as low as the left shoulder. Again, just the reverse of the regular head and shoulders pattern where the right shoulder was not as high as the left, indicating weakness. But in this case the right shoulder is not as low as the left, and this is indicating strength.

Just as the previous pattern fell below support of the neckline, this inverted pattern breaks out above the neckline, advancing.

Now look at the lower right side of the chart at the volume. The increased volume during a breakout above prior resistance is very important. Volume confirms as it did in the break down in the earlier pattern.

If a breakout above a known resistance level occurs and there is no increased volume, be very skeptical. Sometimes a false breakout occurs and the price retreats back below the resistance level. Most every time, false breakouts are on low volume.

Now let's take a closer look at the Inverted Head and Shoulders Pattern.

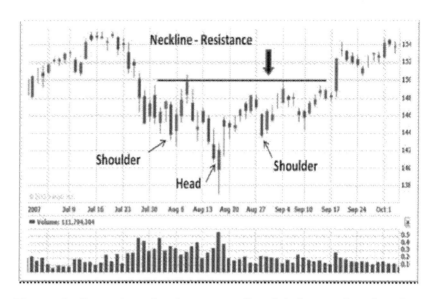

First of all, notice the long candlestick immediately after the lowest point of the right shoulder bottom. Once the stock traded down to the low of the right shoulder, it opened higher the following day and traded up to close, forming a positive candle. Three days later it hit resistance at the neckline, pulled back for four days, and then made another attempt at a breakout. It finally breaks out and closes above the resistance of the neckline. That should be a lesson to you as to the power of resistance. This stock finally broke out above it, but unless a stock has the momentum, or sufficient buying interest, always recognized as 'volume' on the chart, they usually cannot break out. That is why volume is so important.

This is classic of a stock that had to 'prove itself.' Meaning, it simply had to trade above the lowest low long enough to garner the momentum to move higher. When you think about it, there were obviously enough buyers to provide support, but after it traded above support for a few days, more buyers became convinced the support was going to hold and they began buying.

Once again, this is a very accurate way to forecast what is likely to happen in the future, just like we learned previously studying the chart of the DJIA. In this chart above, you can see how the Head and Shoulders pattern is formed by the price action of this particular stock.

While it was trading continually at the resistance level, that indicated a break out was a 'probability,' then the close above the resistance finally confirmed it. To enter a position on this stock, a good entry point would have been after the confirmation close above the resistance level.

But it is always wise to wait for the breakout, make sure there is increased volume, and then enter. That way you are entering just above known resistance, the old resistance is now support, and you can place your stop loss just below the new support level. A very low risk entry with a high potential for profit, and that is key. This type of entry is always the best. You are entering close to known support, placing a stop loss just below that support, and minimizing any loss. Your risk is low, your potential loss is minimal, and your profit, or reward, is high.

Always buy very close to support. That way your maximum loss is very small. Always use a stop loss, and let the stop loss do the work for you in case the stock turns and heads back down.

# *Double Tops and Bottoms*

Another one of the reversal patterns is the Double Top.

## *Double Top*

You will see this more often than most other chart patterns since many times a stock, and/or the market will try to make a new high but be unable to. The selling pressure becomes too great and a decline ensues. A double top is identified by two prominent peaks. Double tops and double bottoms are also called an M and W because of their shape.

See Figure 11-4 below.

The inability of the second peak to move above the first peak is the first sign of weakness. It was unable to make a 'higher high,' so the second peak was the first 'lower high.' When prices then decline and move under the middle trough, the double top is completed.

Remember the change in trend? When the price is making higher highs and higher lows, then the uptrend is continuing. But when the higher high cannot be reached, then the trend most usually is changed to the opposing direction.

**Ah! We have much to learn here.**

You will see this pattern many times. The Double Top is just the reverse of the Double Bottom.

What happened with this stock? Yes, it made a high around $140 and then pulled back. And yes, it found support around $118, and then advances again.

But then what happens? It could not make it back up to the previous high. Once the first high was formed, a resistance line could then be drawn at the top. This lets you know when the stock attempts to move higher it must break that resistance to do so. This one couldn't do it. That is your first red flag. No higher high and a red flag if you are holding this stock in your trading account or your portfolio.

It then pulls back to the support and that doesn't hold. That's a huge red flag. The angle of advance is something worth noting and remembering as well. When a stock price advances creating an angle on the chart greater than 45 degrees, it is not sustainable. Reaching the first high was a sharp advance and that usually indicates euphoria. Euphoria never lasts very long in the market, and certainly is not something that will sustain a stock's price.

If you are holding this stock, these warning signs are what you are looking for after an advance. When the second high is lower than the first, this is when you should have your stop loss tightened up, take some money off the table, or both.

Once it falls through support, this is when a worried investor or trader still hanging on starts pulling up charts for 6 months or a year back to see where the next support level *might* be. That is *not* a position you want to find yourself in. Watching your money evaporate while trying to figure out where the stock might have support and then calculate how much you'll likely lose by the time support is reached.

Please note: This is *not* just for the trader. A passive, buy-and-hold investor who fails to sell when the stock breaks support is facing a huge loss to the investment account. There is never any guarantee where support will be found; therefore there is no way to even estimate the loss, other than 100%, of course. Sure, one could pull up a chart covering 1 year, or maybe 5 years and try to get some idea where support might be found. But why risk your money? Especially if support is $10 or $20 per share lower.

This is for every person who trades or invests. This is a perfect example of what can happen when you blindly buy any investment without protecting your capital with a stop loss.

The buyers at $135 are probably still licking their wounds years later. Once again, need I remind you, who sold out at $135, and who bought at $135? Once again. we see Distribution.

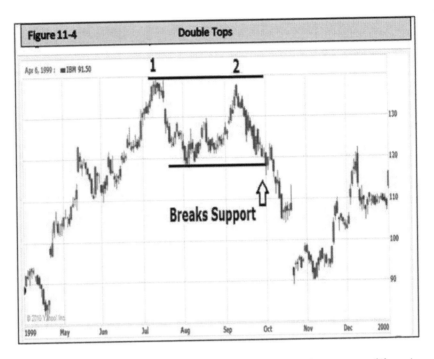

Figure 11-4 Double Tops

Someone bought that stock at the top, *not* even waiting to see if it could move above the previous high or push to a new high. They bought their shares blindly, hoping it would go up, possibly without even placing a stop loss...

Look at the huge Gap in the above chart. Imagine the novice that bought at $135 and is still holding on, hoping it will go back up so he/she wouldn't lose so much money, and all the sudden, the market opens and this stock gaps down another $10. True, you can't do anything about a gap down. That happens before the market opens for trading. But an astute investor would have already been sold out before that gap occurred.

## Put it in perspective:

This is a great example of how quickly losses can happen and how devastating they can be. In this example, we are not looking at a chart of a fly-by-night dotcom stock. This is IBM. If the investor just owned 100 shares and purchased them at $135 per share, or $13,500.00 – At the close of the market the day before the huge gap down, the investor was already down to $10,700.00 ($107 per share). Then the market opens the following day and immediately is down another $10 per share ($1000). So in reality, this investor is now down $3800, close to a 30% loss in a matter of about 30 days.

**Let me just say this:** You are *not* smarter than the market. None of us are. That's why you can never just buy something because it might look good and *hope* it goes up in price. When a stock or index breaks a support level, there is a reason for it. You may never know the reason, and it really doesn't matter if you do or not. What matters is, you must listen to what the market is *saying!* In this particular stock, it couldn't make a higher high – red flag number one – it then fell below the previous low breaking support – another red flag.

A reasonably tight Stop Loss would have sold you out near the top around $130 per share and you would still have $13,000 in your account, instead of holding on to watch $40 per share disappear from your investment account as it fell to $90 ($9,000). Always think *risk vs. reward* when entering any trade or investment. You must always protect your capital at all times. Otherwise you are risking it all for whatever reward you might get. Those are not great odds.

Another note about Gaps:

This chart shows the stock gapped about eight times during approximately one year of trading. All gaps were eventually closed but one. Just like a Gap Up, a Gap Down is often closed as well. In this stock, if you count the daily bars, it took approximately 21 trading days to close that huge gap down. Do you think the novice that bought at $135 held on that long? Probably not... like most novices, they *buy high and sell low*!

Many mistake a gap up in a stock to be a true sign of strength and want to jump in and buy. When in reality, if you jump in, the price will usually fall back to close the gap... In other words, if you chase a stock that has gapped up, you'll likely lose!

I want to make another point about support and resistance with this chart.

See Figure 11-4 with added resistance line below.

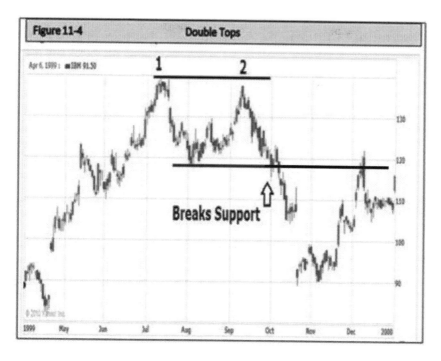

Figure 11-4 — Double Tops

Breaks Support

When this stock traded back up to close that huge gap, look where it stopped. By extending the old support line across the chart, that old support became resistance as the stock traded higher. We see that it had fallen through support at about $119 per share, and then briefly traded back above that same level before declining once again.

On the right side of the chart we see it briefly traded above the old support, now resistance, and then fell back.

That is how powerful support and resistance levels really are.

# Double Bottom

The double bottom is the mirror image of the double top. See Figure 11-6 below.

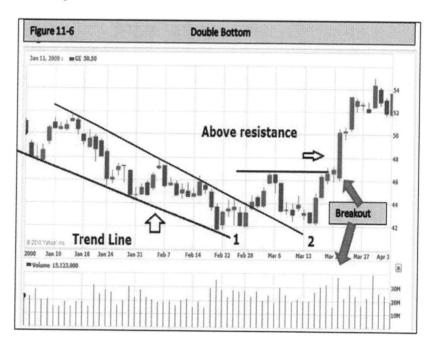

The double bottom is also a very common pattern and very predictable as well. Historically, a stock will re-test the lows, or support. Once a stock declines and finds support, there are obviously traders and investors who believe the company is worth that amount of money, or if it is an index like the S&P 500, then the index is a value at that level, so they buy. These are the first buyers who provide the support. But once the stock trades sideways for a while, maybe advances a little, and then declines again to that level and the support holds, then other buyers realize this level truly is support and are willing to start buying. Thus, an increased number of buyers translates into higher demand and an advance in price. This may mean that the first support was provided by the higher risk takers and the second support included buyers that are less of a risk taker, but the result is the same.

In Figure 11-6 below, we see a clear Double Bottom pattern, and I have also added a Trend Line to illustrate that the trend lines can be used successfully in a declining market.

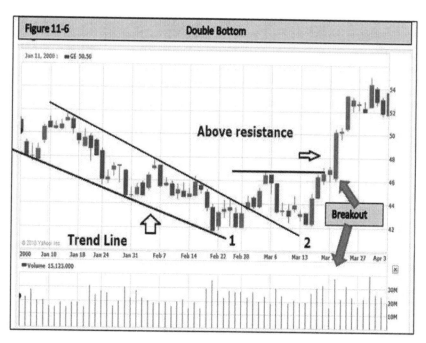

Figure 11-6      Double Bottom

Historically, a stock will re-test the lows much more often than not. This is a signal of strength, and is what normally creates the Double Bottom on the chart.

As the stock is declining, the trend line is followed. But once the trend is broken, as in this case, it didn't make a lower low by trading lower to reach the old trend line, and a new trend begins. By adding a channel line to the declining trend, then you are alerted when the stock trades above the channel, thus indicating a breakout of the declining trend.

## *What does this tell us?*

Re-testing the lows is exactly what happened in this chart. The stock (GE) fell to around $41, found support, traded a little higher, and then fell again re-testing the low.

Interpreting this information tells us a number of things:

1) There is solid support at that price level. It is really not important that we know why. It could be that is exactly what the company is worth. It could be many different things, most of which we will never know. What is important is the fact that the chart tells us that is where there is support. The price is the footprint of money!

2) More importantly, a buying opportunity exists when the low was re-tested and held. This is confirming there is support at that level. Remember, buying

close to a support level and placing a Stop Loss just below known support is a very low risk trade and the most opportune time to enter. You would be risking a minimal amount with an opportunity for a very high return.

3) The second low was slightly higher than the first. That is also a bullish sign. This means that buying interest is solid, more buyers have entered, and selling has waned.

This information is invaluable. You will see this pattern develop on numerous charts. When you see a stock that has traded down to a low, keep this pattern in mind. Watch the stock to see if it re-tests the low. If it does, and it holds, then you have a great buying opportunity.

A seasoned trader will wait for the stock to find support, and most usually will wait for confirmation before stepping in. He won't be buying at the top, he will be selling. He buys at the bottom, and only then once he is reasonably certain the support is going to hold.

Another important factor shown on the above chart is the breakout above resistance was on increased volume. Not only is the volume confirming a move higher, it also tells us there are other traders and investors who have waited for the breakout to buy the stock.

A good entry point could have been after the formation of the Bullish Engulfing candle at the second low. By purchasing at that point around $45 per share, the next high was near $55 per share, which is a $10 per share gain. Not bad for a 10-day investment. That translates into a little over a 20% gain with your money at risk for only about 10 days. Then, sell and wait for another opportunity while the money is sitting safely in the account avoiding any risk.

Another point I should make here:

Many do not realize there are experienced traders and speculators that wait for years for the opportunity to step into the market and take advantage of a major upswing. They will not risk their money unless there has been a serious decline in the market and as some say, 'buy when there's blood in the streets.'

I am not saying everyone should be an active trader. But the above chart is a classic example of a Trend Trader's dream. Their money sits in the account safe from risk, drawing a little interest, while waiting for a low-risk/high-reward opportunity. Once a pattern develops on a chart that they recognize, then they enter carefully with a Stop Loss to limit any downside risk and take advantage of the up-side potential.

Conversely, a buy-and-hold investor has 100% of their investment dollars at risk 100% of the time. I cover this in detail in my book, *'Trading the Trends.'* But over the past 100 years there has been a Bear Market on the average of every 3.5 years. So the buy-and-hold investor takes an average hit of 29% on the portfolio on average of every 3.5 years and then spends another 1.9 years waiting to just get back to even. Not necessarily a smart money decision!

In summary, a key factor in trading short-term, or investing long-term, is waiting for the set-up, waiting for the right opportunity. Jesse Livermore is regarded as one of the greatest traders of all time because of his trading success in the early 1900s. He once commented, "*You don't make money by trading, you make it by sitting.*"

What he meant by that statement was simple. It takes patience to wait for the trade to develop, for the opportunity to present itself. Let the market *come to you*, instead of chasing the market. Chart patterns are very accurate. They have proven their accuracy and predictability time and time again, but you have to wait for them to develop.

The point is, you might see a stock trading higher and be tempted to buy. Or you may see a stock decline and it may appear it has reached a support level. But you still have to wait for a pattern to develop that you recognize. For instance, in the previous chart when the stock made the first low, it would have been tempting to jump in and place a stop loss just under that level. And that time, it might have worked out fine. But the safer and better trade would be to wait for support to be tested, the double bottom pattern to form, and then enter.

Of course, for the investor who wants less risk, waiting for the breakout would also be an option.

# CHAPTER 11

## *Saucers and Spikes*

These two patterns aren't as common, but are seen enough to certainly warrant discussion. The *spike* top (also called a V-reversal) pictures a sudden change in trend. See Figure 12-1 below.

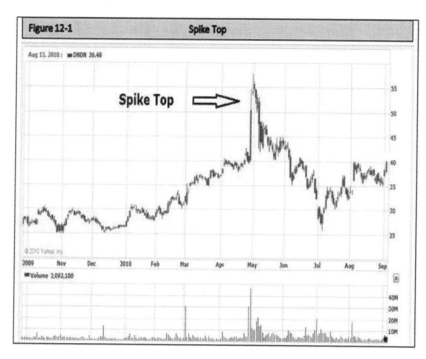

Figure 12-1      Spike Top

What distinguishes the *spike* from the other reversal patterns is the absence of a transition period, which is sideways price action on the chart constituting topping or bottoming activity. This type of pattern marks a dramatic change in trend with little or no warning.

As you will learn, it is certainly not something you want to buy into. When you see one of these forming as the price increases dramatically, it's not the time to buy. If you own the stock, it's generally the time to sell!

In the above chart, you can see the gradual, healthy advance from February to May, and then a sudden advance of $15.00 per share in the stock price, only to return to the trading range and then decline further.

There are several things that can cause this to happen. Many times you will never know the underlying cause. It could be a short squeeze or any number of things. That's really not important. What's important is what you do when it occurs.

- If you own the stock – **sell on the way up!**
- If you don't own the stock – **stay away from it!**

When a stock is running up, take your profit. Don't try to guess where the top may be, because the chances of you guessing it right are slim and none. Another thing to consider is this. If you own the stock and actually hold it through a spike top or bottom, it is usually wise to exit at the earliest opportunity. This is because the stock has now shown it has the tendency to react this way, and eventually you will get caught on the bad side of a reaction and it will cost you dearly. Sure, it's nice to see a dramatic increase in price, but the next time may be a drastic drop instead.

Another example in the following chart shows both the Spike Top and Spike Bottom.

See Figure 12-2 below.

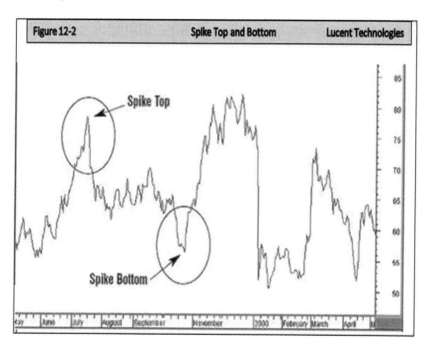

You can see in the above chart a Spike (Blow Off) top. This rapid advance in the stock price obviously came with little or no warning. No warning is customary in these types of scenarios. You can see the stock (LU) was in a steady uptrend pattern then over a period of a few weeks advanced from the $60 range up to around $80. Then just as quickly fell back to the previous trading range in the $60 neighborhood. This stock, as I remember well, was the 'Darling' on Wall Street. It had been in a constant uptrend, and everyone wanted to own this stock.

There are several things that can cause these sudden advances and declines. However, the most common cause for the advance is likely **short interest** and/or a **short squeeze**.

For example, this stock had been on a steady uptrend and as you can see on the chart prior to the rapid advance; the price reached the $65 range. A short squeeze can happen when a number of traders sell the stock short thinking; in this case, it is overpriced at $60 to $65. They possibly think it would pullback and they could make a quick profit on a correction in the price.

They are short the stock, anticipating a decline, or even just a pullback, in the price. If the stock pulled back as they anticipated, they would purchase the stock back at a lower price to cover their short position making a profit on the difference. However, the stock starts advancing. Keep in mind, the more the stock advances, then the greater the loss for anyone who has sold the stock short.

Therefore, as the stock advances, the short sellers begin to buy the stock to cover their positions and minimize their losses. So as they buy, their buying adds to the price increase. And this usually happens rapidly because in the event a trader is trading on 'Margin', a sizable

decline in his account will result in a *margin call*. This
would force the trader to either purchase the stock to
cover his short sale at a loss, or he would be required to
deposit funds into his account to cover the margin
requirement.

So it becomes a squeeze, known as a *Short Squeeze*.
The trader has few choices.

This scenario can also be caused by a large investor,
such as a Hedge Fund, who sees the short interest in the
stock and begins buying and as the buying continues, the
price increases, thus, forcing the Short Sellers to buy and
cover their positions. Of course a Hedge Fund would
most likely begin buying to try to initiate the rapid price
increase and then be selling to the short sellers who are
forced to buy at the very top while causing the short
sellers to suffer a loss.

Let's look now at the Spike Bottom in the previous chart.
First of all, this particular stock is all over the chart.

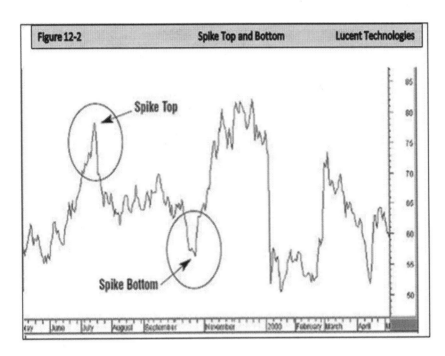

**Figure 12-2** | **Spike Top and Bottom** | **Lucent Technologies**

**Let me just give you a warning.** It is best to avoid this type of stock activity, and/or a stock that has the tendency to fluctuate like this. It is almost impossible to be on the *right* side of the trade. Eventually you will get caught and lose.

You can see that the stock price has returned to the $60 trading range after the Spike Top. Then suddenly the price takes a dive. What causes this?

If you look closely, the stock had *some* support around $64 per share. Most traders and investors will place a Stop Loss just under a known support level in the event the stock breaks below support. This is very wise, and is something you should always do. A likely scenario in the above chart is the stock price fell below the $64 area where many had thought would be support. As the price declined below the anticipated support, the Stop Loss orders began automatically selling.

As the stop loss orders are filled, the price continues to decline. Short Sellers see this, and immediately sell the stock short to capture a quick profit on the decline. This creates even more decline, and more stop loss orders are executed, thus causing further, and rapid, decline in the price.

But then a sudden reversal begins when the stock price reaches a level that many perceive to be a bargain for the stock, and they start buying.

Once the stock price has found a bottom, then demand overtakes supply, and the reversal is in place. This is almost the same scenario as the Spike Top. The Short Sellers must buy to cover their positions and capture their profit, and when they do, their buying once again causes the price advance. At the same time, while the short sellers are buying, other investors who believe the stock is oversold are buying and the rapid price increase moves the price back to the area of the trading range.

If you get caught in this scenario, there are a couple of things you can do.

Number one: As I mentioned previously, you should avoid stocks with this nature. However, let's assume you own a stock, and see a rapid increase in price. You are holding this stock and see the price has increased dramatically in a short period of time.

You would have choices:

1) You could do nothing. Just wait for the stock to return to normal.

2) You could sell for a very nice profit. Then wait for the stock price to recede and re-enter the position. But as I said, owning a stock of this nature is not necessarily a wise thing to do.

So realistically, it usually is wise to take a profit and stay out.

The Spike Bottom is also a problem if you own the stock. Mainly, because the drop in price will occur so rapidly that you won't have the opportunity to get out. However, you should always have a stop loss in place to protect you from losses in the event something like this happened.

But if you were caught holding the stock, you would most likely decide to sit and wait for the price to return somewhere close to normal, and then decide whether to close the position or not.

You usually never know what caused the sudden drop in price. If it was bad news from the company, such as missed earnings, a lawsuit, or something similar, then the bounce back in price might not happen very soon. But generally, after a drastic drop in price, if only due to the Short Sellers covering after the decline to reap their profits, this will usually cause at least some bounce back in the price. A bounce back in price can be your opportunity to exit the position.

A Spike, or Blow-Off Top, is *not* limited to an individual stock or security. The overall market can do this too. Albeit, it generally takes longer periods of time for the Market as a whole to reach a Spike Top, and the spikes are not as sudden. But I am sure you remember the market fiasco of 1999 through 2000 as the Dot-Com craze came to fruition. "What goes up – Must come down."

That being said, you should always remember the 45 degree angle. Any advance in a stock, index, or the market in general at more than a 45 degree angle on a chart is a warning sign. Most generally it is euphoria buying and time to tighten up the stop losses and prepare for an inevitable correction, and possibly even a severe decline such as a bear market.

Spike tops and bottoms are **never** buying opportunities. This type of chart pattern is a warning, not an opportunity to trade or invest. Let others risk their money by trying to pick a bottom when the stock is dropping like a rock. Let them 'catch that falling knife.' Your money is much safer in your account. Your decisions to enter the market should be based on careful thought and patiently watching for the lowest risk opportunity.

In summary, stocks that have a tendency to move up and down rapidly, and without notice, are stocks to avoid.

Leave these types of trades for the inexperienced trader and investor who want excitement and the chance to hit it big with a huge over-night gain. They might get lucky and make big money once in a while, but they won't be around very long because their money will be gone.

Short term profits made off of wild trading stocks always evaporates rather quickly.

You want to be methodical. Make your decisions slowly and patiently. You are not looking to make a few bucks on a quick move in price. You are looking to make big profits on a much larger move in the overall market. And to do this, you must wait for the opportunity to buy at the bottom, protect your investment capital, and then take your profit at the top after a sizeable gain.

## The Saucer

The saucer, in contrast to the spike reversals, reveals an unusually slow shift in trend. Most often seen at bottoms, the saucer pattern represents a slow and more gradual change in trend from down and sideways, to up, eventually. The chart picture resembles a saucer or rounding bottom—hence its name.

See Figure 12-3 below.

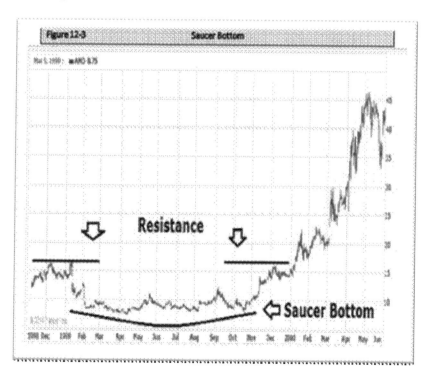

Looking at the chart you see little price movement during the formation of the Saucer. For almost a year the stock stays in the $10 trading range with very little variation in price. Notice two peaks during this time period. It looks like it tried to muster up the energy to advance, but simply didn't have the momentum to do it. Owning a stock like this will put you to sleep. However, this is a perfect type setup to put on your stock alerts.

For instance: If you are perusing stock charts and see a stock in this formation. You might want to set an alert to notify you if the stock 'breaks out.'

In this particular case, an alert could have been set for $18 or $20 dollars. Just above the last known resistance. Then if the stock hit that price you would be alerted that a possible break out was happening. At that point you could wait for confirmation, check the volume on the breakout, *and then buy*. The confirmation would be a close above those peaks in the center of the rounded bottom. Therefore a close in the $20 range on good volume would confirm that the break out was in place.

The small peaks in the middle of this saucer formation are really what most would consider false breakout attempts. Sure there are those who might have bought the stock at the bottom, around $5 per share, and got lucky when it advanced a few bucks and took a quick profit. But until a stock like this can trade above the last known resistance, it is just treading water. Another thing to consider is the stock's price. A $5 stock is normally not a strong stock that everyone wants to own. It is barely above the penny-stock value and most of these do not have the buying interest to make significant advances. In other words, when there are no buyers, there's no advance.

# CHAPTER 12

## Continuing Patterns

Continuing patterns are just that... A continuation of the current trend.

## *The Symmetrical Triangle*

Instead of warning of market reversals, continuation patterns are usually resolved in the direction of the original trend. Triangles are among the most reliable of the continuation patterns. There are three types of triangles that have forecasting value. They are symmetrical, ascending and descending triangles.

Although these patterns sometimes mark price reversals, they usually just represent pauses in the prevailing trend. Many times they are formed by a consolidation period. Meaning, the stock may have advanced, but instead of a more serious correction, it just goes into a more sideways move and consolidates. This is a time when the stock holders are really not interested in selling. Therefore the volume is light while the stock price consolidates. There are a few short-term traders who may be taking their profit and moving on to greener pastures, looking for something that's moving a bit faster. But for the most part, the investors are satisfied to continue to hold their positions.

The *symmetrical triangle* (also called the *coil*) is distinguished by sideways activity with prices fluctuating between two converging trend lines. The upper line is declining and the lower line is rising. Such a pattern describes a situation where buying and selling pressure are in balance.

See Figure 13-1 below.

Figure 13-1 — Symmetrical Triangle

Somewhere between the halfway and the three-quarters point in the pattern, measured in calendar time from the left of the pattern to the point where the two lines meet at the right (the *apex*), the pattern should be resolved by a breakout. In other words, prices will close beyond one of the two converging trend lines.

You will see this pattern during upward trends. It is like the stock has moved up from a lower price level, and just needs to 'take a breather,' so it pauses and consolidates.

Notice the higher lows during the formation of this triangle. That indicates the uptrend is still in place, but simply doesn't have enough momentum yet to move higher.

While watching one of these patterns form, there are several things that cross the mind of a trader.

First of all, early on when the price moved up to around $50 the second time, but didn't reach the previous high, the first thing that would come to mind as a trader/investor would be "that is a double top." But the stock pulls back and holds above the previous low, so there is no reason to sell since the last known support (the previous low) held. In fact, it made a higher low which is good. The only problem at that point is the lower high it made. But then it advances again and makes another lower high. At this point, with two highs and two lows, a trend and channel line can be drawn creating the triangle. At that point most traders are going to wait to see if a break out occurs before buying, or a drop below the last support occurs before selling.

That explains why there is less buying on the advances, thus the lower highs. It just becomes a waiting game. They are not going to buy without a breakout and certainly not going to short sell a strong stock that is making higher lows. But see what happened as soon as the stock advanced to break out above the old previous high? Yes! It 'Gapped' up the next day.

The buying interest returned... Look at the volume on the breakout as well. The higher volume tells us that there were many traders and investors waiting for the breakout.

Do you see that the 'Gap' at the breakout was closed a few days later? It took a week or so, but the stock traded back down to where the gap occurred to close it. You can also see that there were several gaps on that chart, and most were closed. That is just something to keep in mind. More often than not, gaps are closed.

## The Ascending Triangle

The *ascending triangle* is very similar to the *symmetrical triangle* with a rising lower trend line, except it has a flat upper channel line. An *ascending triangle* pattern always appears that buyers are more aggressive than sellers since the lower trend line is rising and the upper channel line is flat. So this is usually a bullish pattern.

See Figure 13-2 below.

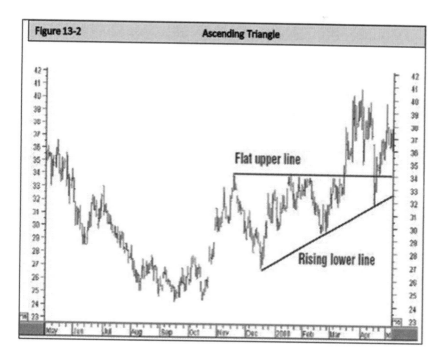

You can also see the lower trend line could have been drawn from lowest low around $25, connecting the lows each time there was a pullback. Therefore by the time the stock broke out above the upper channel line, it had already found support along the trend line the fourth time.

**Here is an Exercise for you** – count all the gaps in the chart above. I counted 8. See if you find them all.

Notice that they were *all* closed, except for one and if it wasn't, it was extremely close to being closed. That is typical; gaps are usually closed more often than not.

## The *Descending Triangle*

This looks similar to this Ascending Triangle, except the descending triangle has a declining upper channel line and usually a near flat lower trend line. This would indicate that the sellers are more aggressive than buyers. So this is usually a bearish pattern.

The descending triangle usually forces a trader to *wait and see* what will happen. But the formation itself suggests it is bearish. Although there are no lower lows being made, it is just holding support. In the mind of a trader, the lower highs indicate weakness, and each lower high suggests more weakness. So it always appears it is just a matter of time until the support fails to hold.

Realistically, the stock only has two options. It either has to eventually break out above the declining channel line or fall through support. And the lower highs tell us the selling pressure is becoming stronger. So it becomes a squeeze.

Talking about Trend Lines, Descending lines, Ascending lines, Flat Bottoms, Bullish and Neutral, etc, it may get rather confusing. But when you look at the formation of a Triangle Pattern, the "Descending Triangle" having the flat bottom would tell you that the Buyers are *not* that excited – if they were, the bottom would not be flat – It would be ascending. Therefore it is a weak pattern that may not have the strength or momentum to advance.

Yet the symmetrical and ascending triangles are showing strength with the higher lows. Therefore, they are more likely to be advancing.

Another way to look at, and interpret a triangle is this: When you look at the wide end of the left side of a triangle, and then follow the lines to the point (Apex), it becomes rather obvious that *something* has got to give. It's like squeezing a juice box from the bottom up. The more pressure that is applied, the more likely the juice is going to squirt out the straw.

That is why when the bottom trend line of the triangle is in an upward trend that is a pretty clear indication that the buyers are more aggressive. And eventually they are likely to win the battle and the price will move higher.

Yet, when the bottom is flat, the buyers are not as aggressive; they are just holding and waiting. There are possibly a few new buyers that are buying at the support, but even those buyers are waiting for the stock to reach the support before buying, thus, no higher lows.

In the above chart, you can see when the stock finally broke below the support, many of those who were holding and waiting suddenly became sellers. This caused a dramatic drop very quickly, not to mention other traders who jumped in to short-sell the stock. But you can see there are about three daily candles just under the support level. This tells us that there would have been time to exit the position once support was broken before the stock eventually fell by $10 per share or more.

The point is, the use of a stop loss would have prevented a huge loss by selling you out quickly. If your stop loss was just under the support level – you would have been sold out and avoided the loss.

## *Flags and Pennants*

These two short-term continuation patterns mark brief pauses, or resting periods, during dynamic market trends.

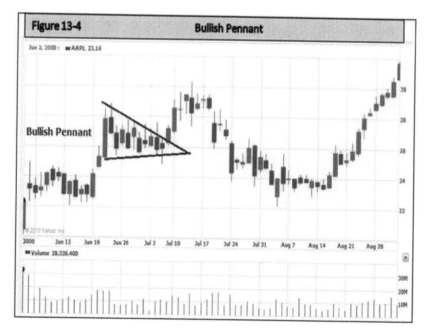

Figure 13-4      Bullish Pennant

Both are usually preceded by a steep price move (called the *pole*). In an uptrend, the steep advance pauses to catch its breath and moves sideways for two or three weeks. Then the uptrend continues on its way. The names aptly describe their appearance. The *pennant* is usually horizontal with two converging trend-lines (like a small symmetrical triangle). The long bullish candle that started the pennant is the main difference between a pennant and a symmetrical triangle.

Notice something very important about the above chart on Apple.

Starting on the left side of the chart, notice the volume on the up days, and the declining days, etc. The important factor here is the volume was always confirming the move, whether up or down. On the days the stock made a big move up, the volume increased. And during sell-offs, the volume declined.

This tells us that this is a *healthy* advance. When the stock was moving sideways or declining, the volume was light. And on advances, the volume was heavy. Also note, I am not suggesting that Apple is a great stock to trade. There have been times in the past that the opposite was true.

I am simply pointing out that a stock that has a high volume of trades per day, and is in a steady uptrend should look like this. It should not have the wide swings that we have seen in other charts we have discussed.

Wide swings are great if you are on the right side of the trade. Day traders love those. But drastic moves are incredibly difficult to trade. You might be right occasionally, but the few times you are wrong will take all your gains.

# *Bull Flag*

In the following chart we see what is called a Bull Flag. This is another continuation pattern.

See Figure 13-5 below.

We also see another stock, like the previous one, methodically advancing with very few pullbacks. And if you connect the lows with a trend line, the advance is likely a little less than a 45 degree angle.

Bull Flags are short-term patterns that slope against the prevailing trend. This is a minor trend within the primary uptrend. The uptrend usually resumes after the upper line is broken.

This particular chart is really not all that exciting. But I want to point out a couple of important things.

Basically, this pattern is given the Bull Flag name mainly due to the tall pole that formed at the top of that advance, and this pole can be either a solid candle or a wick. A very important thing to remember is that just because you see a 'pole' form at the top of an advance, do not assume it is a Bull Flag. You must wait for the formation.

Wait until you can be reasonably sure that a pullback has taken place and the price has found support and the advance is likely continuing.

Note: I want to start introducing you to 'reversal bars.' We will study them in depth later, but you need to start being able to recognize them.

Look at the bottom left area of the chart where the price had declined for about eight days and then formed the bar at the lowest point. Notice the open and close for that day were virtually the same price. Meaning the stock price didn't fall further, yet didn't advance either.

This tells us that the buyers and sellers were very evenly matched that day. The significance is that this happened *after* a decline. The DOJI at the end of a decline or at the end of an advance is a very good indicator that a change in trend is coming. But don't forget the key word here is *after* an advance or decline.

**Reversal Bars are important.**

When seeing this at the time it was happening, your very first thought should be that it is a *reversal bar*. It formed after the decline, and suggests that the stock is going to change directions. On this chart there are three declines. A *reversal bar* ended each of the declines and the stock began another advance.

Figure 13-5 — Bull Flag

Now look at the very top right side. After the advance, there are four reversal bars. An indication that a change in direction is about to happen, which in essence, is exactly what it did.

# CHAPTER 13

## *Price Gaps*

We have already discussed price gaps to some extent, but let's explore them a little further. Gaps are simply areas on the chart where no trading has taken place. Simply, the stock opened for trading either higher or lower than it closed the previous trading day. Not only are they normally filled, or closed, they can also provide very significant bits of information as well.

An upward gap occurs when the lowest price for one day is higher than the highest price of the preceding day. A downward gap means that the highest price for one day is lower than the lowest price of the preceding day.

Therefore, a gap is nothing more than the result of the price of the stock being either bid *up*, or bid *down*, prior to the market opening for trading that particular day. Generally it happens because of news. For instance, a company may have released a report causing traders to believe the stock is suddenly worth more or less than it was the day before. If the earnings for the previous quarter had significantly increased and were much better than expected, the stock price may Gap up. And conversely, if the company reported disappointing earnings, this may cause the price to Gap down at the opening of trading. As we learned in chapter one, this is directly related to the market factoring in, or *discounting everything.* There are many other factors that can cause a gap, but as I said, it generally is news related.

You have obviously seen that there are Gap ups, and Gap downs. As I have pointed out many times, Gaps are normally *filled.* Why?

Let me give you a little more understanding of gaps, and at the same time answer the question of why they are filled. To do this, I need to give you a better understanding of *who* sets the opening price that causes a Gap Up or Gap Down.

Remember, whether you are trading, or buying as an investor for the long term, gap trading is risky business, and the specialists who mark stocks up or down prior to the open of the market have a vested interest in doing so.

A market maker (specialist) is the professional on the trading floor of the exchange who makes his/her living buying from, and selling stocks to the public.

A market maker is *also* the professional on the trading floor whose job is to provide liquidity to the market. This means that the market maker is obligated to buy and sell the stocks that he/she provides a *market* for.

For instance: One Market Maker may provide a market for only one stock. And that Market Maker is obligated to buy and sell that stock to and from the public in order to provide liquidity, a balanced market, and this allows the public to always be able to buy or sell that stock, at *some price*.

A Market Maker (Specialist) is also responsible for managing large movements by trading out of their own inventory. If there is a large shift in demand on the buy or sell side, the specialist will step in and sell out of their inventory to meet the demand until the trading gap has been narrowed. This adds liquidity, and keeps the market flowing smoothly.

Now, if you were a Market Maker, providing liquidity to the market, where would you open a stock for trading with poor news, knowing you would be receiving *sell* "market on open" orders? (Sell orders for that stock at the *market price* at the open of the market for trading that day)

You would open them as low as possible, (where you felt the stock was well supported and would have buying interest). In other words, you might be the one buying these shares and you want to buy at a price level that you feel you can sell at later, profitably.

This is known as 'buying weakness.' Conversely, with strong news on a stock, knowing you would have 'Buy Orders' at the open, and you, as the market maker, would be selling at the open, where would you open the stock for trading?

As a market maker, you'd open that stock at as high a level as possible (to enable you to sell stock to buyers at would-be resistance levels).

This is referred to as 'selling strength.' This is why gaps have a greater propensity to close immediately after the open. Thus, many gaps do not show on the charts because they are closed within the first few minutes of trading.

This is why I never recommend buying a stock at the 'market price' as soon as the market opens if the stock is gapping up for the day. Simply because, many times the gap up will close within an hour after trading begins, and if you placed a buy-at-open order, you might be paying the highest price the stock traded for that day, only to watch it fall back to close the gap.

Let's look at the different types of gaps that appear at different stages of the trend. Being able to distinguish among them can provide useful and profitable market insight.

Two types of gaps actually have forecasting value:

1. Breakaway gaps
2. Exhaustion gaps.

A breakaway gap usually appears at the bottom, close to the beginning of an advance. An exhaustion gap can be at the top after an advance or at the bottom near the end of a decline. Some will claim that a gap in the middle of an advance, referred to as a measuring gap, or runaway gap, indicates the trend is about halfway through its cycle. But I have never felt that type of gap had very much forecasting value.

See the common gap in Figure 14-1 below.

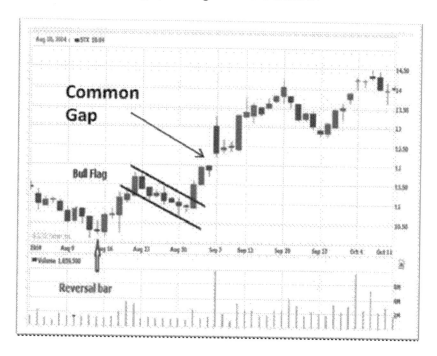

The gap in the above chart was created just three days into the advance, and would be referred to as a breakaway gap. The presence of this gap does indicate there is momentum and buying interest and would certainly be something to watch if you were interested in the stock. Obviously, you would want to wait to see if it was filled, and then enter a position. Otherwise, if you tried to enter on the day of the gap, you might be entering at the top of a near-term high and support would be several dollars away. That is not a good entry point, ever. You always want to buy at support, or very close to it.

In the following chart there are many different types of gaps.

See Figure 14-2 below.

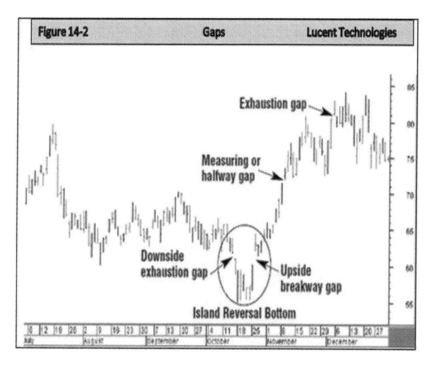

First, let's look at the gaps at the bottom of the chart that created the island reversal. Sometimes an exhaustion gap is followed within a few days by a breakaway gap in the other direction, leaving several days of price action isolated by two gaps. This market phenomenon is called the *island reversal*, as seen on the above chart, and usually signals an important market turn. Unlike most other gaps in trading, these gaps are not normally filled. The island reversal is not that common, but it can happen after a significant decline.

The **breakaway** gap usually occurs upon completion of an important price pattern and signals a significant market move. For instance, a breakout above the neckline of an inverted head and shoulders bottom or after a double bottom pattern has formed would be a time a breakaway gap might occur.

The *runaway* gap usually occurs after the trend is well underway. It often appears about halfway through the move (which is why it is also called a *measuring* gap since it gives some indication of how much of the move is left.) During downtrends, the breakaway and runaway gaps usually provide support on subsequent market dips. However, if the stock falls below the gaps, then during up-trends these two gaps act as resistance during any rallies or bounces.

The **Exhaustion Gap** is one of the most telling, and occurs right at the end of the market move and represents a last gasp in the trend. In the above chart we see an exhaustion gap at the top of the advance and at the bottom. When they appear at the top, you should think *euphoria*. Most often, that is exactly what it is. If you own the stock you should be looking to exit. If you don't own it, then don't consider buying it at the top unless you really enjoy losing money.

Exhaustion gaps are different than the other gaps, mainly because of the reason for the gap. At the top, the reason is unrealistic, and based on false hopes and dreams. At the bottom it is because those same hopes and dreams are vanishing, very rapidly.

Exhaustion gaps are primarily psychological. What you must realize is the fact that trading and investing involves money, the trader or investor's own personal hard earned cash. The thought of losing this valuable asset, and/or the thought of making a lot more of this valuable asset is highly emotional, and therefore is always psychological.

So a Gap up after a stock has already been advancing in price is based on *hopes* that the stock is going through the roof. That the proverbial 'Train is Leaving the Station' without the last buyers. The problem is, a professional would never *throw money* at a stock in that situation.

Let's look at an exhaustion gap at the bottom.

See Figure 14-3 below.

This is a classic exhaustion gap. The stock has declined for more than 30 days from a high of about $44 to close one day at $32. Then it gaps down the following day, and this is indicative of *throwing in the towel*. Those who bought this stock at, or near the previous high, hung on during the downtrend hoping it would reverse, and when it looked like it was never going to turn around, they threw in the towel.

Also notice the heavy volume on the day it gapped down. This is typically referred to as **'Capitulation.'** Capitulation is a cleansing, so to speak – getting rid of the last of the sellers. The price didn't decline further and that tells us there were buyers at that level. But the sellers didn't know that. When the market opened that day, the stock had already been trading in pre-market at a discounted price, it was obviously gapping down, the bids were low, and buyers were scarce. So they sold out to avoid more losses.

The buyers who stepped in were obviously professionals. They knew where support was and were ready to buy the bargain once the stock traded down to that level. More than likely, they were also the ones selling at the $44 level when all those reversal bars were forming.

That is why knowing where support and resistance are, is such a valuable tool. It is a must for every trader and investor.

While we are on the subject of gaps, the most common cause of a gap up is news. Normally either after the market closes one day or before it opens the next, news hits the air waves and causes either a gap up or a gap down, obviously depending on whether the news is good or bad. Many times gaps are caused by investment firms raising their rating on a stock. I'm sure you've seen it on the news or in headlines from time to time.

> **HEADLINES:**
> "XYZ Investment Firm raised its rating on XZY Company to a Strong Buy!"

Never buy a stock based on some investment firm raising their rating. Never, ever…

Many times this type of news will create buying interest in a stock and cause a gap up. Don't ever buy it at the open, and possibly not ever. Always wait for a chart pattern to form that you recognize before you buy anything.

Believe it or not, Investment firms release news like this to create buying interest to help support the price of the stock so they can unload that stock from their inventory. It happens more often than you could imagine. As a Day Trader, using a Level II trading platform you can see the market live. You can see who is buying, who is selling, etc.

I have seen countless times an investment firm continually selling a stock after releasing a news report about raising their rating. They were never on the 'Buy Side' all day. They were just filling orders all day, unloading.

Yes, this is a feeble attempt at market manipulation. But they do it all the time. When you think about it, it really is not much different than Talking Heads proclaiming the DOW is going to 20,000 when reaching its all-time-high. Many guests on the financial networks do the same thing. Seldom will you ever see a guest that is not bullish on the market.

Point is: They have a vested interest. Money...

**What should you do with a GAP?**

For instance: Let's say you have been watching XYZ stock, you have done your proper research in studying the charts, past history, price movements, etc. You now feel this stock is a buy at this level. But you notice that the stock is gapping up when the market opens.

**Number One**: You should *never* simply place a 'Market Order' to buy a stock, and then leave for work knowing that it will be bought for you at the market price when the market opens. This could get the stock purchased for you at the *high* of the day, and then the price retreats, closing the Gap, and never advance to the price you actually paid. As you can imagine, there's nothing quite as discouraging than starting a trade off with a loss.

If you cannot watch the market prior to placing your order, then at a minimum, place a "Limit Order" to buy. Meaning, as an example: you would specify on your order to buy at $25 or better. This way if the stock gapped up, opening at $26, your order would not be filled until the stock price came back down to your entry price or lower. Using the previous day closing price would be a good point – that way if the gap was closed that day you would be buying at the bottom of the gap. This would increase your chances of being profitable in the event the gap closed and then the price began an advance.

A Limit Order can also be used to sell, in the event you were ready to sell a stock, and it was gapping up, or down.

Hopefully what you have learned regarding gaps will help you when you are faced with either buy or sell decisions during a gap situation.

Most importantly, don't chase a stock either up or down. Wait for a pattern to form that you recognize and then enter safely.

Let's now look at the very important areas of key reversals, retracements, volume, how to spot them, and their importance.

# CHAPTER 14

## *The Key Reversal Day*

A price formation we are always watching for is the *key reversal day.* This minor pattern often warns of an impending change in trend.

The trader is always watching for indicators that a trend may be about to reverse, both, in downtrends and up-trends.

- If you are holding a position, you want to protect your gain.
- If you are looking to enter a position, you are looking for a reversal from a downtrend or pullback.

Sometimes the key reversal day is blatant and very hard to miss. Especially when you see one of those long negative engulfing candles form at the top of an advance, or maybe a long positive candle at the bottom following a decline. But sometimes recognizing the key reversal day is not some magic candlestick that forms, but a minor pattern. It can also be a matter of where it forms, such as a DOJI forming at a known support or resistance level.

The following chart clearly shows the spinning top at the very peak of the advance indicating a reversal may be about to happen. Then the all important confirmation came the following day with the bearish engulfing candle.

So in this case, the spinning top was a forewarning of things to come. It formed after an advance, and then the engulfing candle was confirmation.

That one is pretty clear. However, there were several early warning signs. See the long-legged DOJI 5 days prior to the start of the decline? Then there is the hanging man the next day, and then a negative candle, a shooting

star, and finally the spinning top. The trading Gods are
pretty liberal fellows, but they normally don't give a trader
that many chances to exit a position and avoid a loss.

Another point I should make about that chart is the stock
actually advanced out of the Bullish Pennant and tried to
move higher. It just didn't have the momentum to carry
through.

You will see this happen occasionally. After a sell-off, a
bounce ensues. In this case it was a false breakout. It
broke out through the resistance of the downward sloping
upper channel of the Pennant, but the volume was low,
and within a week it headed south.

Let's look at some more reversals. In the following chart
you can clearly see a change in trend.
See Figure 15-3 below.

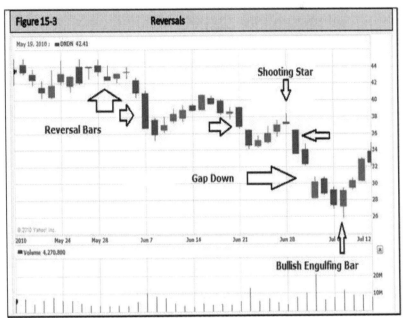

Figure 15-3           Reversals

On the left side of the chart at the $44 level there are a number of candles indicating a change is coming. There's a Bearish Engulfing candle followed by a Hanging Man, then a day later a Shooting Star appears, then a day after that a DOJI shows up to the party. It's a little hard to miss all those warnings. But we do know there were buyers. And a couple of days were positive. So obviously there were those that were ignoring the warning signs. But that's always the case.

During the decline there were a couple of little rallies. The first one ended with a Bearish Harami formation and the second ended with a Shooting Star.

I realize it's easy to analyze a chart after it has formed. I also realize it is a bit more difficult to apply the

information in real-time. But to make it easier, it is always best to use a trend line whether you are trading short-term or long-term. In my book, **Trading the Trends**, I enter and exit trades using trends and technical analysis. But I will give you a lesson here as well.
See Figure 15-4 below.

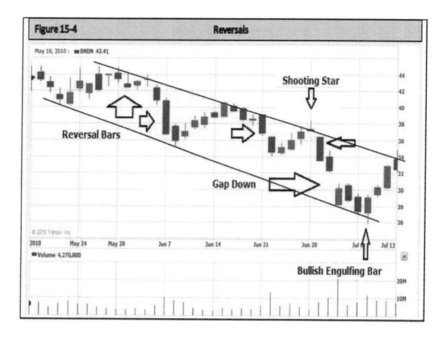

By using two highs and two lows, you can draw a trend and channel line and extend them to the infinite. And with these lines in place, it is almost expected what the stock will do when it advances up to the channel line or drops to the trend line. The point is, if you have a channel line drawn and the stock reaches the channel line and forms a DOJI, a Shooting Star, or any other warning signal, you already expect it. The warning makes more sense. This technique works in advances as well as declines.

In the above chart, once the channel line was drawn after the first two highs, the next time the stock reached the channel line and formed that shooting star, you wouldn't even be surprised. You might even consider selling it short. This, by the way, is exactly what active traders do. That is how they find their entry points to sell short on a declining stock or the overall market.

Now back to the reversals. In the above chart the first minor rally began with a Bullish Harami. This is the formation with a small positive candle following the large negative candle, and the small positive one being within the trading range of the large negative candle.

The second rally began much the same way and the third rally began with a large bullish engulfing candle.

Yet the third and the fourth rallies traded right back up to the upper channel line. That is not a coincidence. Stocks always trade within a range, or channel whether they are in an advance or in a decline.

When watching for reversals, there is usually a bit of anticipation. Common sense tells us that nothing goes up forever, and it also tells us that most stocks will find support somewhere above zero. So we normally anticipate a pullback or correction after an advance and we anticipate a rally after a decline. So it becomes a matter of recognizing the early signals as to when the anticipated change may occur.

In the following chart, there are several early warning signals we need to discuss.

See Figure 15-5 below.

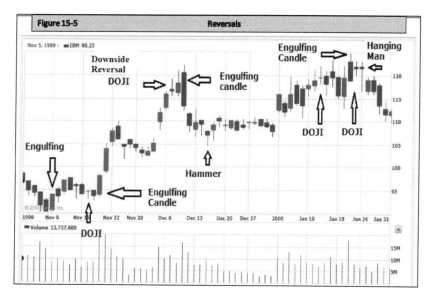

Starting in the lower left corner, we see a decline was ended by a large positive engulfing candle. Those are hard to miss. But after a small rally another decline begins. The first signal before the huge advance was a DOJI. Two days before the stock advanced about $3 in one day, the DOJI was signaling a change in trend.

Now look in the upper center of the chart where the arrow is pointing to the long Engulfing Candle where the actual reversal happened. I want you to notice the bar 2 days prior to that big down day. It is marked DOJI with an arrow.

*That* is your warning! Yes, the big reversal day didn't happen until 2 days later. But the DOJI is your warning when you see that bar form at or near the top of an advance, you should consider yourself warned that the 'winds of change' are blowing.

Let's pretend for a second that this chart is forming in real time. In the picture below, I've cut off the right side of the chart and the last thing you can see is the DOJI that has formed at the top of the advance.

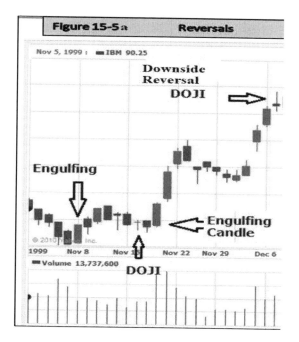

As a seasoned trader, you would be expecting a pullback even as the DOJI forms, why?

The 'Gap'... The Gap in price three days earlier had not been filled. Since gaps are normally filled, this one should be no different.

Now look at the area on the right side of the chart showing the other engulfing candle that was a downside reversal day.

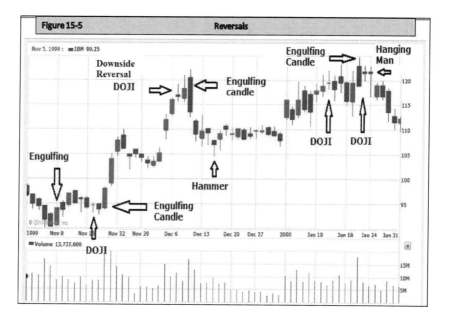

Can you find your early warning?

Yes, it is five days before the big down day indicated by the large engulfing candle.

There are actually three warnings on that reversal besides the big down day. The one I already pointed out five days before the big reversal day, and two immediately after, which were a spinning top and a hanging man. Either of those would be a warning signal, but in this case they are both there.

Let's continue with the same chart.

See Figure 15-6 below.

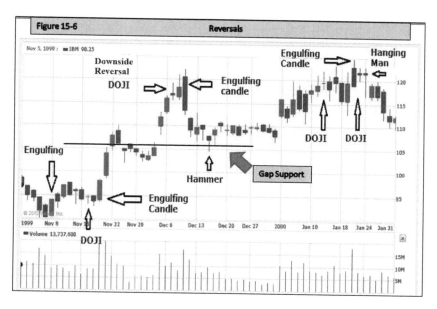

Notice that I included a support line. This support was created by the gap up. Even though the stock traded back down to close the gap, the gap provided support. The lower side of a gap is normally former resistance and we see the stock traded up to that level, crossed it once and fell back, then traded up to it again before gapping up above it.

I didn't include the lines, but you can see when the stock gapped down after the first large engulfing candle, that gap was then resistance at the $110 level for about three weeks of trading before finally gapping up above it. Then that same gap provided support as we see the wicks of the candles trading down to it several more times.

I also want to mention the hammer that formed in the middle of the chart. This reversal day candle is one of the best at forecasting that support has been found and a reversal is looming. Simply, the formation of the candle tells us that the price opened that day, declined, thus causing the long wick on the bottom of the candle. Yet the buyers stepped in causing the price to return back to close very near where it opened.

Not only does this tell us the buyers and sellers were closely matched that day, but when this candle forms after a pullback or decline, it is a strong indication that the buyers are at least as aggressive as the sellers. This type of aggressive buying is very significant. And when it happens after a decline, it is a very good indicator of trend reversal.

# CHAPTER 15

## *Reversals*

**The obvious and the not so obvious.**

Sometimes reversals are very obvious. Like some we have already discussed, the following chart shows the classic reversal candles that you should be looking for.

See Figure 16-1 below.

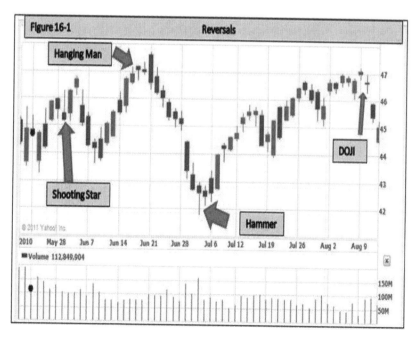

As you can see, following an advance or a decline a very obvious candle is formed that gives us a good idea about the future trend.

At the top of the advance in the above chart, the Hanging Man and the Spinning Top are almost dead give-a-ways. The hammer at the bottom is a pretty clear signal as well. Then when you look at the right side of the chart, after about a 30-day advance, the DOJI is pretty obvious that a correction may be in store.

But what about when there are no clear signals?

Take a look at the following chart.

See Figure 16-2 below.

Sometimes there are just no signals for entry. In the above chart, besides the one funny shaped candle at the bottom that kind of resembles a hammer, that's about it until you get to the top of the chart nearly sixty days later. All the way up is just a bunch of DOJIs, spinning tops, and various other mismatched candles with no confirmation the following days to indicate a change in direction.

This is one of those times if you didn't get in at the bottom when the hammer was formed; there just weren't any pullbacks to form a known support to enter. Nothing recognizable and it happens sometimes. In a case like this, about the only way to enter is, once there are two little pullbacks, draw a trend line and use it to find an entry point by waiting for the stock to trade back to the trend line.

In doing so, there must always be a tight stop loss. Because there is always the chance the uptrend could change and head back down to test the low at the funny shaped hammer.

Now, at the top, once the stock had advanced for nearly 60-days, there is a large negative engulfing candle followed by a shooting star and a hanging man. These three candles are definite early warning signs. So a short seller might be licking his chops waiting to sell the top and ride it back down. There is close to a $10 advance and if the stock only had a 50% correction that could be a nice quick profit.

But to be safe, after a healthy advance like that, a trader would be wise to wait for at least a down day on heavy volume before shorting a strong stock.

Let's take a look at another not so obvious pattern. See Figure 16-3 below.

In the chart above, the tops are not too difficult to recognize. Simply notice the spinning top on the left top that formed or the engulfing candle on the right top. But the bottom is messy. The very bottom has a resemblance of a DOJI but with a long wick extended up. There are up days, down days, and then negative days when it actually advanced by opening higher (gapping up) and then trading back down.

The point to this is simple. There is not always a recognizable reversal candle or pattern. Sometimes the market is just not tradable. Sometimes there seems to be no rhyme or reason to the movement. Those are the times it's best to watch, learn, and plan. Keep your money in your pocket. Wait for a clear signal. Wait for a pattern that you recognize to form and then enter safely. Trying to enter at times like those in the above charts is risky business. You might get lucky, but you might lose. It's just not safe. So remember the phrase, "when in doubt, stay out."

There is another tool that can be very helpful at times. That tool is to look at the big picture. That is something you should always do anyway. But instead of focusing on a small time frame, expand your chart and look at the big picture.
See Figure 16-4 below.

In the above chart, I simply expanded the previous chart back in time to cover about four years and I highlighted what is shown on the previous chart in the top right corner.

Now, that crazy trading in the previous chart makes a bit more sense. By looking at the big picture we see the stock has been in an uptrend for 3 years, is trading at the top of the trading range up close to the upper channel line, and is probably due a serious correction.

You see, before making any trade or investing in any stock, the big picture is **always** the first place to look. At market tops, stocks become more volatile, more uncharacteristic, and much more difficult to trade. This is because they may be entering the distribution phase of the market cycle.

I can't express strongly enough the importance of this one technique. The big picture is always very telling. It will provide insight and prevent you from making huge mistakes by buying something at the top only to either get stopped out, or suffer a huge loss. This stock was trading at about $45 per share and the lower trend line was $10 per share below that. Buying up there is asking for a $10 loss or several small losses while buying dips and hoping you found the bottom only to get stopped out every time.

When stocks pullback or go into a correction, you must always have a good idea as to how much of a correction is healthy. Whether you are a short-term trader, or a long-term investor, this information is valuable. For instance, a 10% correction might not be too much of a concern to a long-term investor. But a 50% correction will get their attention in a hurry.

## *Percentage Retracements*

Let's discuss percentage retracements. Market trends never take place in straight lines. Most trend pictures show a series of zigzags with several corrections against the prevailing trend. These corrections usually fall into certain predictable percentage parameters.

Historically, the market has shown to move in either 3-day or 5- day increments.

Meaning, in an uptrend, the market historically has either three days advance before a slight pullback, or five days advance before a slight pullback. The same holds true in a declining market. Meaning, you will normally see either three days or five days down before a bounce back.

A key indicator in studying this is the amount of retracement that the market, and/or a stock, retraces after an advance or decline.

The best-known example of this is the **fifty-percent retracement**. That is to say, a secondary, or intermediate, correction against a major uptrend often retraces about half of the prior uptrend before the bull trend is again resumed.

This tells us that if your stock is in an uptrend, then after a decline, it advances $5 in price without a pullback, then during a pullback, it should retrace no more than about 50%, or $2.50.

Retracing more than 50% after advancing is a sign of weakness and at a minimum should be noted and watched closely.

Bear market bounces often recover about half of the prior downtrend. A minimum retracement is usually about *one-third* of the prior trend. The *two-thirds* point is considered the maximum retracement that is allowed if the prior trend is going to resume. A retracement beyond the two-thirds point usually warns of a trend reversal in progress.

What does this information tell us? We should always remember what goes up – must come down! However in this scenario, we are expecting slight declines along the way as our stock advances.

You just learned how much you should expect without panic or fear. This is also helpful in setting your Stop Losses. During an advance, by using a 50% retracement amount you can calculate where the price should stop and resume the advance. Thus, you can set your Stop Loss just below that price in case of a significant decline.

The key is always the *prevailing trend*. In an uptrend you can calculate the likely retracement, or correction, after each advance. But keep in mind, during a Bear Market the prevailing trend would be down. So the retracements would be bear market bounces. Some might be 30%, some might be 50%, but do not confuse a simple bounce as change in trend.

## *The Interpretation of Volume*

Volume tells us a story too. It's like the Great Confirmer. Remember, Charles Dow considered volume as a confirmation of a change in trend.

Chartists employ a two-dimensional approach to market analysis that includes a study of price and volume. Of the two, price is the more important. However, *volume* provides important secondary confirmation of the price action on the chart and often gives advance warning of an impending shift in trend.

You will become accustomed to looking at a chart, and in a matter of seconds, recognize any significant pattern, and then *check the volume*. We have studied Reversal Patterns which include Double Bottoms, Double Tops, Head and Shoulders, etc. Volume tells us if it is significant. Volume tells us if it is possibly 'real' or sustainable.

For instance: When we discussed Break Outs. When a stock advances above a previous high, we call that a 'Break Out.' However, without significant volume, it is likely to be a False Break Out.

Take a look at the following chart.

See Figure 17-1 below.

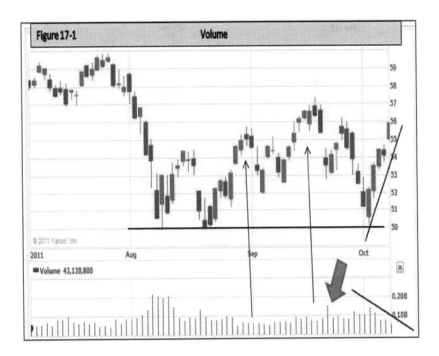

Figure 17-1    Volume

Notice how the volume is the confirming factor. The decline on the left side is on heavy volume as the stock traded down to support. The first bounce was very light volume, yet the volume increased on the following 3-day decline. The third bounce advanced to $57 per share but there was no volume. The immediate decline following that bounce shows almost double volume. The last advance from support on the right side of the chart looks impressive until you look at the volume moving lower every day.

Volume must always confirm the move; whether that move is up, down, a break out, or simply a healthy advance.

The wider the day's range and the heavier the volume, the more significant the warning becomes and the more authority it carries. Meaning, if the trading range is wide, then the move is significant. Conversely, if there is heavy volume and little movement, then that forms a DOJI and tells us the buyers and sellers are closely matched.

Volume is the number of units traded during a given time period, which is usually a day. It is the number of common stock shares traded each day in the stock market. Volume can also be monitored on a weekly basis for longer-range analysis.

When used in conjunction with the price action, volume tells us something about the strength or weakness of the current price trend. Volume measures the pressure behind a given price move. As a rule, *heavy volume (marked by larger vertical bars at the bottom of the chart) should be present in the direction of the prevailing price trend.*

During an uptrend, heavier volume should be seen during rallies, with lighter volume (smaller volume bars) during downside corrections. In downtrends, the heavier volume should occur on price selloffs.

For instance, Bear Market bounces should, and usually do, take place on a lighter volume.

**Volume Is an Important Part of Price Patterns**

Volume also plays an important role in the formation and resolution of price patterns. Each of the price patterns described previously has its own volume pattern. As a rule, volume tends to diminish as price patterns form.

The subsequent breakout that resolves the pattern takes on added significance if the price break-out is accompanied by heavier volume. Heavier volume accompanying the breaking of trend lines and support or resistance levels lends greater weight to price activity.

See Figure 17-2 below.

The volume is confirming the price moves.

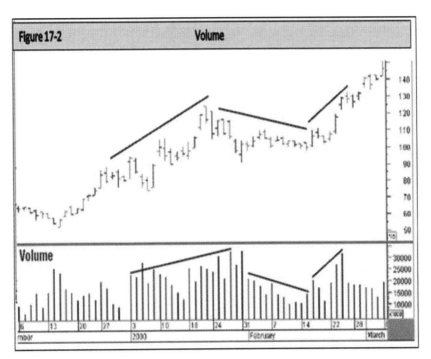

# CHAPTER 16

## *Moving Averages*

Moving averages are extremely popular with market technicians and for good reason. Moving averages smooth out the price action and make it easier to spot the underlying trends. Precise trend signals can be obtained from the interaction between a price and an average or between two or more averages themselves.

The moving average is constructed by averaging several days' closing prices, however, it tends to lag behind the price action. The shorter the average (meaning the fewer days used in its calculation), the more sensitive it is to price changes and the closer it trails the price action. A longer average (with more days included in its calculation) tracks the price action from a greater distance and is less responsive to trend changes. The moving average is easily quantified and lends itself especially well to historical testing. Mainly for those reasons, it is the mainstay of most mechanical trend-following systems.

## *My Personal Favorite*

Yes, I always use moving averages. They work well whether you want to be in the market for long periods of time, short periods of time, or even if you want to trend-trade the market. And, they are available on virtually any charting software, even the free ones like Yahoo Finance.

Securities prices, market indexes, and mutual fund prices vacillate up and down from day to day, week to week and month to month. Because of this it often becomes difficult to discern which way the prices are actually moving. A moving average is therefore used to smooth the data so that the trend can be easily detected. A rising moving-average line indicates that prices are trending up, while a declining line indicates the opposite. A flat line indicates a market stuck in a trading range and can't seem to make up its mind which way it is going.

The following chart (Figure 17-4) is a five year chart of the DJIA with a 200 DMA. The moving average is the solid line shown on the chart.

Figure 17-4

You can create a moving average of any length (e.g., 10-day, 20-day, 50-day, 200-day) and for any time period (days, weeks, months) depending upon what you are trying to achieve: for example, for trading the market over short time frames a short time-frame chart would be used with a short moving average. On the other hand, investing for the long term, a long term chart would be used with longer term moving averages.

Referring to Figure 17-3 below, you can clearly see the concept of using moving averages.

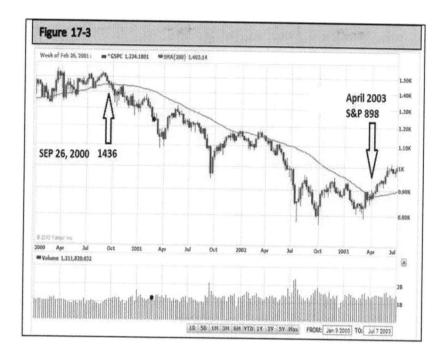

Figure 17-3

Many traders and investors use the moving average to help find entry and exit points. Some even use the 100 or the 200 DMA as signals to buy and sell. Meaning, the moving average is used to find points to exit the market or enter the market.

For instance, when the S&P 500 index price crossed below the 200 DMA you would have sold and got out of the market on September 25, 2000, missing the 609-point drop from 1436 to 827 in September 2002. During this period of time, the S&P 500 only penetrated the 200 DMA a couple of times in early 2002. The moving average confirmed this was a down-trending market, even if it had not been declared a Bear Market while the chart was forming in 2000. Still, by using the moving average, you would have known that the stock was trading under the moving average instead of on top of it. Thus, signaling a break down, and the potential of a downtrend beginning to form.

Some investors use a crossover strategy. Meaning, they might consider it a sell signal when the 50 DMA crosses over the 200 DMA to the downside. This action is commonly called the 'death cross.' It signals very weak market internals when the 50 DMA crosses below the 200 DMA, so they sell and go to cash.

Conversely, they would buy when the 50 DMA crossed back over the 200 DMA on the upside.

Some of the more popular time periods used by market professionals for moving average crossovers are the 20-dma, the 50-dma, 100-dma, and the 200-dma. Keep in mind when investing using moving averages for buy and sell signals, it is critical to select a moving average that is not too sensitive to "whipsaws." Rapid upswings in price above the moving average only to soon reverse and fall below the average, and to downswings which can do the same, first falling below the moving average and then soon turning up above the average.

This situation is most common during a market that is trading sideways in a trading range. Also, be aware that the shorter the time period chosen the more subject you are to whipsaws and false breakouts, while the longer the time frame the slower the signal, meaning that you will miss a part of the move that had already begun. So, the time frame you will most likely choose will be relative to whether you are trading with a short-term or a long-term objective.

## 200 DMA vs. 50 DMA

The 200 DMA is considered the one most indicative that a real market trend is in place because it covers a period of 40-weeks worth of trading. In the next two charts, Figure 17-5 you can see that the 200 DMA is slower moving and farther away from the prices, while in Figure 17-6, the 50-day is a tighter fit.

Figure 17-5

Looking at Figure 17-6 you can see that the 50 DMA tracks closely to the prices and would have had many buy and sell signals, whipsawing back and forth.

Figure 17-6

If you are using the moving averages as buy and sell signals, you must be especially careful in a sideways market because too many buy and sell signals often lose money during trading ranges. For the long-term investor, in a sideways market you are better off in cash. The reason is, you do not know which signal will work out beforehand, so you have to take all of them. Otherwise, you do not have a strategy. You should never take some signals and avoid others. That is a path to confusion, loss of discipline, and ultimately, financial ruin.

However, using the 200 DMA alleviates many of the signals and protects your investment capital.

Losing money some of the time is an integral part of any trading system if it is to work. You just need to remember to limit your loss on each trade with a stop loss, and if you are stopped out, just sit tight and wait for the next signal before you jump back in.

The Following Chart is the DJIA 5-year with a 200 DMA. This chart was pulled direct from Yahoo. These charts are free – easy – I simply chose a five year candlestick chart for the display and then selected a 200 DMA to be added to it.

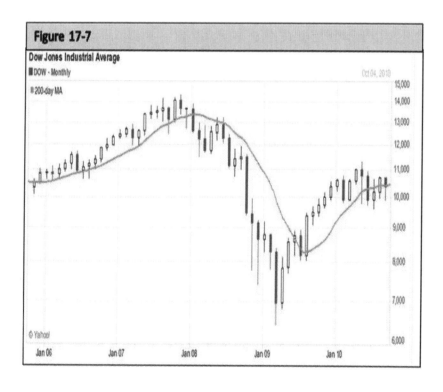

Figure 17-7

This is a true learning experience. It covers five years of investing, and tells us many things.

**First:** Look on the left side of the chart in December 2005 and early January 2006. Notice that the DJIA crossed the 200 DMA and not only stayed above the moving average, but the moving average was in an upward trend, slanting upward, for almost two years. Historically, the 200 DMA serves as 'support' for a stock or index price, and also resistance if the stock or index is trading below the moving average.

This is clearly shown on the chart from Jan 2006 to Jan 2008 each time the DJIA traded down and touched the 200 DMA it turned and traded higher. Also note that the price penetrated the 200 DMA on three occasions during that time and actually traded higher each of those times to close above the average.

**Second:** Look at what happened in January 2008. This Bearish Engulfing candle is particularly important because not only does this candle normally signify a change in direction of the market or a particular stock, in this case it also crosses and closes below the 200 day moving average. In the preceding weeks the market had reached an all-time high, and over the previous two years, each time the market had penetrated the moving average it had still moved back to close above the average.

But in January 2008, this particular week was conclusive evidence that there was possibly a change taking place. Also note, that is the point that the 200 day moving average changed directions. From this point the moving average turned downward and the market began trading below the average.

Now bear in mind, as the chart was forming, the 200 DMA would not immediately turn downward. So the astute investor would have only the bearish engulfing candle that closed below the average as the signal to move to safety. Even if the investor waited for the next candle to form for confirmation before moving to safety, he still could have preserved massive gains and avoided a more than 50% loss.

Another important thing to remember is that the market or an individual stock will normally not trade too far away from the moving average. This is to say, that if a stock or the market moves too far above or below the moving average it will generally trade lower or higher at some point in time and return to the moving average.

In the following chart the 50 DMA is also included. The 50 DMA has a lot more zigs and zags, but at times can still be helpful in deciding when to be in or out of the market by using some common sense in your investing.

One thing of importance to note is that in January 2008 the 50 DMA crossed below the 200 DMA, and this is referred to as the Death Cross. Consequently, this happened at the same time the bearish engulfing candle formed.

As you look at the chart above, you can see that by using a 50 DMA, there were very few times that it would give you a clear signal to buy or sell. At the same time, a five-year chart is not necessarily the best to use making more immediate type decisions. Yet it is a great tool to see the general direction of the market.

**Figure 17-8**

The following chart covers only six months.

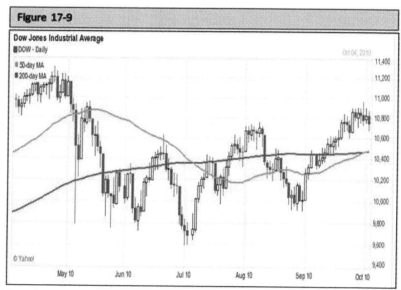

Figure 17-9

Dow Jones Industrial Average

For the shorter term trader the 50 DMA provides a pretty clear picture as to which direction the market *may* take, in the near term, of course. For instance, as you can see in the above chart every time the DJIA moves away from the 50 DMA within a short period of time it will either move up or down to return to trading close to the average. During this six months time from April 2010 to October 2010 the DJIA crossed the 200 DMA several times. And as I have already pointed out, each time it trades higher or lower away from the 200 DMA, at some point it will again return to the average.

How can this be useful to the individual investor?

As you can see in April 2010 the DJIA was trading considerably higher than the 200 DMA and is also higher than the 50 DMA. An astute trader would recognize this as it is happening and possibly sell at the top and wait for a correction or pull-back to reenter.

## *Popular Moving Averages*

In stock market analysis, the most popular moving average lengths are the 50 and 200 DMA.

[On weekly charts, those daily values are converted into 10 and 40-week averages.]

During an uptrend, prices should stay above the 50-day average. Minor pullbacks often bounce off that average, which acts as a support level. A decisive close beneath the 50-day average is usually one of the first signs that a stock is entering a more severe correction. In many cases, the breaking of the 50-day average signals a further decline down to the 200-day average. If a market is in a normal bull market correction, it should find new support around its 200-day average.

# CHAPTER 17

## *Stop Losses*

To be a successful investor you must decide on your investing objectives, and then get a strategy that will work for you, and most importantly, establish rules for limiting your losses that you will adhere to. Don't leave it to chance or you'll be left with chump change.

**I can't stress enough the importance of a Stop Loss.**

It is very simple. When you purchase, know exactly what your maximum potential loss will be.

Let's look at an example of a good Stop Loss. We'll use the SPY 2008-09 chart and for the long-term investor who was using the 200 DMA as a signal to buy and sell. As I mentioned earlier, some investors use the crossing of the 200 DMA as a buy and sell signal. In this case, a sale would have been made when the SPY fell below the 200 DMA at $145.79. Then a purchase would be made at $94.77 per share when SPY crossed back over the 200 DMA to the up-side.

Figure 18-1

This is a good example because after the purchase, the price was up and down for a few weeks before advancing.

The key to every trade or investment is to limit your potential loss. In this case the purchase was made at $94.77 and even an 8% loss would have sold you out at $87.18. Therefore, as soon as you made the purchase at $94.77, you should have entered a Stop Loss to sell your shares if the price dropped below, let's say $87. That way the maximum amount you would lose is $7.77 per share. It wouldn't matter then if the SPY crossing over to the positive side of the 200 DMA happened to be a false rally in the market and the price turned and fell back to its previous low of $68.00, or even lower. You are protected and will not lose more than your set amount.

Don't be greedy or scared and enter a Stop Loss for only a few cents below your purchase. Every stock must have some breathing room and you don't want to get sold out senselessly. The 6% to 8% rule has been around for years. There is a reason this amount is used for Stop Losses. Meaning, normally if the price drops more than 6% to 8% then there is a valid reason for that much decline. And chances may be pretty good that it will drop further.

I normally do not allow that much of a loss although that is kind of a standard in the industry. Mainly because I always buy at support, and if the support does not hold, I want out. And, when I buy very close to known support, my stop loss is less than 6% away from the purchase price.

If you are 'stopped out,' then that does not mean you are a bad investor or trader. Remember, no emotion. It would only mean that the purchase was simply made at the wrong time. Losing 6% or 8% is much better than a 30% or more loss.

Another reason I used this chart is to prove a point. For a wise investor who purchases shares of SPY, which is the exchange traded fund for the S&P 500, he has a diversified portfolio of 500 of the biggest and best companies. He does not pay fees to a fund, fund manager, etc. He only pays a commission for each trade.

Now, using the strategy of buying when the SPY crosses above the 200 DMA and selling when the SPY falls below the 200 DMA, look what he would have accomplished. In my book, **Common Sense Investing**, I use this strategy covering a full 10 years of market action. It is successful.

Point is, in that chart, if the wise investor had 1000 shares of SPY, sold them when the sell signal was given as the price fell below the 200 DMA on the left side of the chart, he would have put his $145,790.00 safely in his account to draw a little interest. After the bear market ended 17 to 18 months later and SPY crossed back above the 200 DMA, he could have purchased over 1500 shares at the discounted price with his $145,000 to take advantage of the next advance.

**Figure 18-2**

SPY 2008 - 09

Sold $145.79

Buy $94.77 June 1st

Since SPY bottomed out at less than $70 per share, he avoided a more than 50% decline in his investment account, earned interest on his money during the bear market, then purchased more shares than he previously owned at a deep discount.

Now compare that to the buy–and–hold Investor who owned the same 1000 shares of stock and watched his account value drop from $145,000 to the low of about $68,000 and may wait many years to ever return to net-gain territory.

To take this one step further. Let's assume the SPY returns to trade at $145.00 per share five years later.

The wise investor used his $145,000 to purchase 1500 shares at $94.77. So when SPY advances to $145 per share again, he will have $75,345.00 profit ($145 − $94.77 = $50.23 X 1500 = $75,345) added to his original $145,000 for a total in his account of $220,345.00. However, the buy-and-hold investor will just be getting back to break-even.

Another very useful technique is to make your purchases in increments. For instance, instead of purchasing all your shares at once, make a purchase of about 25% and watch the price for a few days (with a Stop Loss) until there is an advance and then buy some more in increments. This way if your first purchase is at the wrong time and you are stopped out, then you only lost $7.77 per share on a small number of shares.

Of course as the price increases, then you are profitable and can add to your investment, move your stop loss higher, and even by purchasing more you won't lose any of your capital.

Point is, by using simple strategies like the 200 DMA with a stop loss to limit your risk, you can be successful. Stop losses are your insurance to always protect your investment dollars. Now, let's take our previous example using the SPY as the investment and the 200 DMA buy/sell strategy one step farther.

# Trailing Stop Loss

In continuing our previous example, the wise investor re-purchased shares of SPY after the bear market when it crossed the 200 DMA, and placed a trailing stop loss. A trailing stop loss is set to automatically move higher as the stock advances. It can be set to trail at any amount you choose, for instance, maybe $3 below the current price. Thus, every time the stock moves higher, the stop loss moves to stay $3 below the price.

A trailing stop loss is a very good way to capture more profit and protect your investment dollars at all times. In the chart below notice that SPY reached a price above $120.00 per share before dropping back below the 200 DMA and creating a sell point at a price of $109.11.

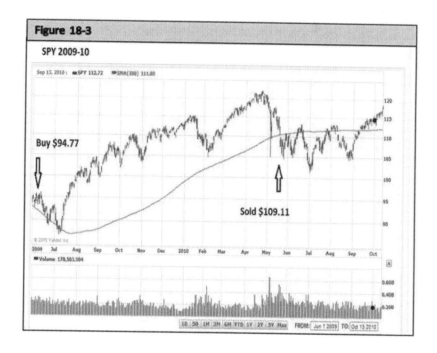

Figure 18-3

SPY 2009-10

Using a trailing stop loss can capture more profit for you when used properly. By automatically moving higher as the stock advances it preserves most of your gain. Yes, you will occasionally be sold out and then have to wait for another entry point. But in the event there had been a Trailing Stop Loss in place as SPY was advancing, then instead of selling out when SPY fell under the 200 DMA, you would have been sold out at a higher price.

For instance, if you felt there was a correction in the market due to happen in the near future since the SPY was significantly higher than the moving average, you might have tightened up your trailing stop loss by setting it at $2.50 below current price, then you would have benefited by capturing more of the gains and been out of the trade quicker.

As you can also see, there are many zigs and zags in the price as it advanced during 2009 and 2010. Yes, a stock can trade significantly above the 200 DMA for extended periods of time, but will eventually return to the moving average. In this case, a trailing stop loss would have worked well keeping it low enough to allow 'breathing room' yet higher than the 200 DMA to preserve as much gain as possible.

## Creative Stop Losses

Don't do it! Many brokerage houses allow Stop Losses to be used creatively. Meaning, they allow you to enter different types of Stop Losses. Such as a 'Stop Limit' order.

These different types of stop losses should be used by only the traders with the ability to watch the market constantly.

To understand how these work, you first have to understand what a Limit Order is, because a Stop Limit Order combines the features of a Stop Loss with those of a Limit Order.

A stop-limit order is practical for the individual investor to use when buying, but not when selling. When you are buying, the order will be executed at a specified price (or better) after a given stop price has been reached. Once the stop price is reached, the stop-limit order becomes a limit order to buy (or sell) at the limit price, which is the price you designated, or better.

For example, let's assume that ABC Inc. is trading at $40 per share and an investor wants to buy the stock once it begins to show some serious upward momentum, as in our examples, maybe crosses above the 200 DMA. The investor has put in a stop-limit order to buy with the stop price at $45 and the limit price at $46.

Now, if the price of ABC Inc. moves above the $45 stop price, the order is activated but NOT filled. Once it is activated, it turns into a limit order, and will only be filled if the price of ABC is under $46 (the limit price). Therefore, if the stock gaps up above $46 to start trading, the order will not be filled. This protects the buyer from purchasing at 'Market Price' in the event the price is much higher than the $46 limit.

The problem with using the 'Limit' feature in a Stop Loss is that the trade is not guaranteed to be executed if the price is outside the limit amount.

For example, let's turn the previous example into a sell situation. If the investor owns ABC Inc. and it is trading at $46, but fears the price is going to fall and used a Stop Limit, then it could be disastrous. If a Stop was set at $42 per share and the Limit was $41 per share, then if the price fell to $42 the Stop would activate, but then the Limit Order would be to sell at $41 or better.

The problem is the limit. If the price gapped down, or fell quickly to $40.75, the order would not be filled even though the Stop had been activated because the price was not above the $41 limit. So the Investor would still be holding the shares until another order could be placed. This can be dangerous in the event a stock or the market is crashing.

A normal Stop Loss order is simple. It is an order that becomes executable once a set price has been reached and is then filled at the current market price. Yes, in crash situations, you might not get a good fill, but you would be out and not holding on to a losing situation. There are ONLY TWO things to remember about a Stop Loss.

1. **USE IT!** Without a Stop Loss you are simply flirting with disaster, and sooner, rather than later, you will find it, or it will find you. When you enter into an investment, place your Stop Loss immediately. Always.
2. **Don't Get Creative**

A very good habit to form is this. If you place your trade online, then *never* get up from your computer after you enter your trade without placing your Stop Loss. The Stop Loss *IS* part of the trade. It is that important.

Regardless, whether you are buying or selling short, a Stop Loss will not eliminate the risk. Risk is always there regardless. But common sense certainly tells us that a Stop Loss will 'Limit' the risk. That is what is important. Always place the *odds* in your favor.

# CHAPTER 18

## *Putting it all Together*

Applying what you've learned is the next hurdle to cross. So let's implement charting principles and technical analysis in some decision making situations. To begin, we must have a stock to trade. I don't normally recommend trading in individual stocks, but if you are inclined to do so, I would suggest either trading small to limit your exposure or day trading so you close your positions at the end of each day. This is because when trading individual stocks, the risk is too high.

Simply put, you might get caught holding the stock when a piece of bad news hits the newswires and suddenly find yourself holding a huge loss. Since bad news normally hits after the market is closed, that means your stock would gap down the next day before your stop loss could get you out without major damage.

So let's use the index fund for the NASDAQ, the QQQ. It is comprised of the 100 largest non-financial companies listed on the NASDAQ. It is not extremely volatile but it still has good price action.

Every trade or investment starts the exact same way. The first thing we must do is look at the big picture. We must know where the stock has been, where it is now, and reasonably predict where it may go in the future.

We'll start with a 2-year chart. That gives us a birds-eye view and a lot of information to work with.
See Figure 20-1 below.

We see the stock has been in an uptrend for more than a year and has now traded down to the lower trend line. It appears to have found support and possibly made a higher low. The correction that started in April from the high of around $50 per share has traded down to the mid-forty dollar range and has provided a good second low for a long-term trend line to be drawn. Note: When drawing trend lines, always use the most significant lows.

Let's use what we know and take a closer look. I always use a 3-month chart as the next step in the decision-making process. A 3-month chart will include most of the minor trends, most secondary trends, and at the same time, the noises of the micro moves are eliminated.

See Figure 20-2 below.

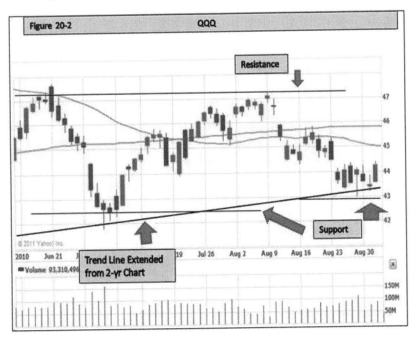

Next, we look for support and resistance. The first rule is to always buy close to support. If a stock is not close to recognizable support, then leave it alone.

I extended the trend line from the 2-year chart and we see the stock apparently found support right on the trend line.

We also see the stock has made a Double Bottom. The second low is higher than the first and that is a positive sign. After finding support at the first low, it traded up about $5 per share to resistance. But now it has traded seven days forming the second low. It first formed a positive engulfing candle, then there was a negative day but it never traded down to the low of the previous day. Then the Hammer was formed. That is a great indicator of a bottom when it forms after a decline. Notice the bottom of the wick on the hammer. That day it traded all the way down to $43 but the buyers took it back up to close positive territory for the day. The spinning top is also very telling, especially when you see the positive engulfing candle the very next day.

Just above $44 per share is a good entry point. According to the closing prices, not the wick of the candles, support is actually at about $43.50 per share. So by entering at $44.50, we are only about $1 away from known support. Support from the previous low is at $42.50, so we are just a couple of dollars away from a second line of support.

Now let's talk resistance. We know there is resistance just above $47 per share, and it has hit that resistance twice. So that resistance is $3 away. The 200 DMA may also be resistance. But we see it has crossed above the 200 DMA two times recently without much of a problem. So that in itself tells us there is buying strength.

Otherwise, it would not be able to penetrate the resistance of the 200 DMA.

So the bottom line is, this is a judgment call. Like most every investment or trade, there are hardly ever any perfect set-ups. But we use the technical analysis tools and knowledge to place all of the possible odds in our favor.

One option would be to wait until the stock traded back above the 200 DMA and even broke above the $47 resistance level. That might be the decision of some low-risk traders. That way, after crossing the $47 level, the old resistance level of $47 would then be support and the stop loss could be placed just below that new support level.

On the other hand, we now have two levels of support just under the current price, positive trading days at the current support level, and three candles that historically are great indicators of a change in trend that have already formed at this support level. Sure, it would be a better trade if resistance was farther away. But we can see that the last rally was a $5 per share move higher, and we also see the prevailing trend is up.

So the downside of waiting for the stock to trade back above the resistance level is at that point it would then be close to the upper channel of the trading range.

Thus, it makes good sense to place the trade now, and then in the event there is a $5 move higher, a stop loss can preserve at least a portion of the gains.

Done!

We now own 500 shares of QQQ at $44.40 per share.

Remember, before leaving the computer, place the stop loss. We have a stop loss at $43.25, just under the last known level of support. So, we are risking only $1.15 per share with a sizable potential gain.

Let's review our trade. We purchased 500 shares at $44.40 for a total of $22,200. With our stop loss just under the last known support level, a $1.15 away, we are limiting our potential loss to $575. If our analysis is correct and the stock moves higher, we will gradually move our stop loss higher as well. That way we will be guaranteed a profit.

Let's see how our trade developed.

See Figure 20-3 below.

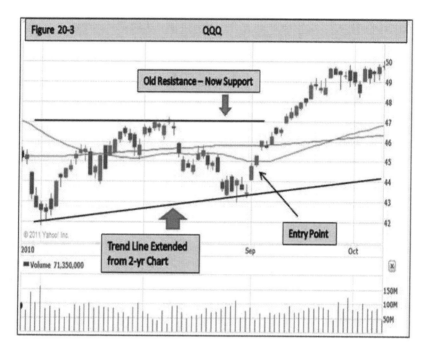

Figure 20-3      QQQ

Old Resistance – Now Support

Trend Line Extended from 2-yr Chart

Entry Point

© 2011 Yahoo! Inc.

2010

Volume 71,350,000

That's how it's supposed to work. A very nice move higher and it only paused one day at the resistance of the 200 DMA and the $47 upper resistance as well. It is time to move the stop loss up. The old resistance at $47 is now support, and a very good place to move the stop loss would be just below the $47 level. That way we are guaranteed a profit and we can let our winner run.

Now, we see it has currently found resistance at the $50 level. So far it appears to be struggling a bit, but there has not been a pullback. So that tells us it is strong enough to possibly stay there at that level until it garners the momentum to move higher. Once it does, then the stop loss would obviously be moved up just below that level.

That is how you manage the trade or investment. You simply watch for pullbacks, new levels of support and resistance, and you move your stop loss up as needed once the stock has traded above those levels.

Obviously, the entry is the key. A good entry will be profitable; a bad one will be a loser. You will never be right every time. But the key factor is to limit your risk by buying close to support. If we had been wrong and lost as much as a $1.50 per share, it would have cost us $750. That may sound like a lot, but put it in perspective. A buy-and-hold investor who buys 500 shares of that stock now while it's trading at $50 per share is risking $25,000. Sure that is the maximum. But what if that stock trades back down to test the low of $42? Then that is a $4000 loss.

But by using our stop loss, we are now guaranteed to make a profit even if the stock declines to $42, or even if it doesn't stop there. We wouldn't care how far it fell, our stop loss would take us out of the trade and our money would be safe in our account. So instead of fretting over a huge loss, we would be patiently waiting for it to find support so we could reenter at a lower price.

Let's use technical analysis to learn when to exit a trade.

We will continue with the same trade. So let's first look at the big picture once again.

See Figure 20-4 below.

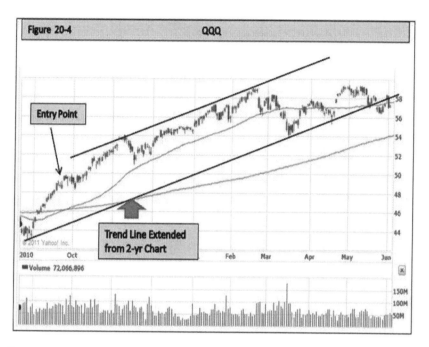

Figure 20-4 — QQQ. Entry Point. Trend Line Extended from 2-yr Chart. Volume 72,066,896.

By extending our primary trend line from the previous charts, we see our stock has continued its advance remaining above the trend.

We also can see that you would have moved your stop loss up to just below $50 once it traded above that resistance. The stop loss would have been moved up once again just below the $54 level after the stock traded back down to the trend line.

But we now see there may be problems ahead. In the last three months it has not been able to trade back up to the upper channel line, and it has now fallen below the trend line. That is not a good sign, so we need to take a closer look.

See Figure 20-5 below.

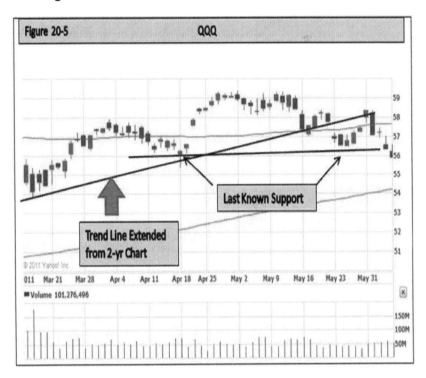

Figure 20-5      QQQ

Last Known Support

Trend Line Extended from 2-yr Chart

A closer look reveals even more concerns. Our stock is showing several signs of weakness.

1. Fallen below the primary (major) trend line.
2. Fallen below the 50 DMA
3. Fallen below the last two levels of known support.

Those are the obvious. But technical analysis also tells some things that are not as obvious. Look at the topping pattern. When it hit resistance at $59 it never traded above that level, not even intra-day, or there would be a candle wick extended higher. Instead, there is a very close trading range each day at the top with spinning tops and DOJIs. Notice the first decline to the 50 DMA, it bounced one day then another DOJI formed. Then it gaps down below the 50 DMA, a sure sign of weakness. The second little bounce was almost wiped out in one down day with the negative engulfing candle, and then it fell below the last known support.

About the only positive sign is the fact it is still above the 200 DMA. But the 200 DMA is right on $54, and that is where the support was over two months ago.

Unless you had a trailing stop loss and were sold out of the trade at $57 or $58 per share, there are only a couple of options here.

1.  Place your stop loss under the support at $54 which was where the stock found support previously. The 200 DMA will also provide some support at that price as well.
2.  Use a trailing stop loss and only give it a short fuse.

It is trading at $56 per share; it has declined for four days, so it may be time for a bounce. So a trailing stop loss with about $1 trigger on it will allow it to bounce if it's going to, and will preserve as much gain as possible if it falls.

I should point out that a long-term trader would have only had to make decisions like this when a problem arises. Meaning, as long as the stock was trading above the stop loss and above the trend line, there was no major concern during minor pullbacks.

But anytime a major trend line is violated, it is a major concern. Even so, with a stop loss, you can let the stop loss do the work for you. You don't have to sit and worry that you are pulling the trigger to sell at the wrong time, afraid that as soon as you sell, the stock will turn and head higher. The decision to protect our capital was made when we entered the trade, and at various times along the way as we moved the stop loss higher.

But let's see what happened. See Figure 20-6 below.

Well, after being stopped out of the trade the stock continued to fall and didn't find support until it reached $53.50. The ensuing bounce went back up to test the resistance at $59 but then the bottom fell out.

As you can see, it is still below the primary trend line. This tells a story as well. Technically, let's see how the dynamics have changed, there is a lesson to be learned here.

1. There is a new lower low. The $54 support did not hold.
2. It made a Double Top. So traders were able to sell that top short for a nice profit on the downside.

There is a valuable lesson on volume.

See Figure 20-7 below.

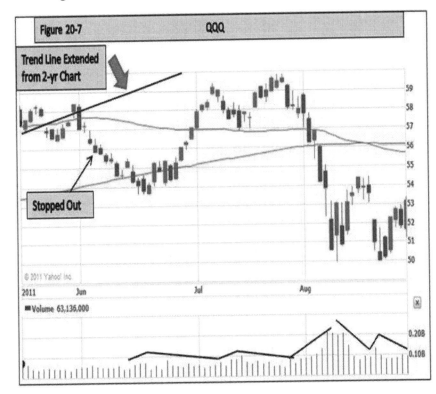

From the bounce beginning at $53.50, notice the declining volume leading up to the high, then higher volume on the next little decline, and then declining volume on the highest high. As you can see, the highs are made on low volume and the sell-offs are on increased volume. This is classic at market tops.

Remember, the volume confirms the trend. Typically, professionals wait for a bounce to sell into the strength. Thus, on the advances, they are not buying, so the advances are not sustainable. There is no volume to sustain the momentum. Yet once a bounce moves the price higher, they start selling again, and so do the short-sellers. The volume increases, and after a decline, the professionals wait for another bounce to sell while the short sellers cover their positions for small profits.

This is why the distribution phase at market tops can take several months to materialize. During the distribution phase, stocks do not make new highs; they are simply sold at the top of every bounce. This continues until the selling pressure finally reaches a point to take the prices down to new lows. In the above chart we see how this stock has already made one new low. But that is likely not the end of the selling.

This is where the chartist draws new trend and channel lines because the old primary trend line has now been broken.

See Figure 20-8 below.

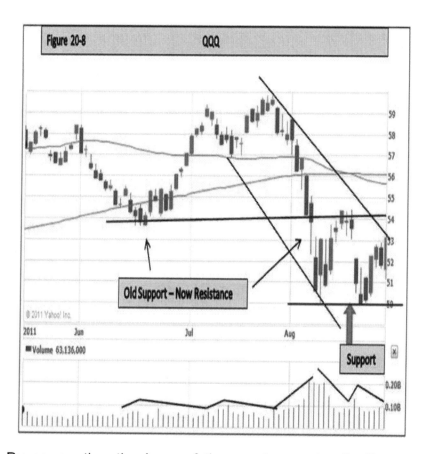

Figure 20-8 — QQQ

By connecting the lows of the most recent sell-offs and connecting the highs of the most recent tops, a new picture begins to emerge.

See how the picture changes once a primary trend is broken? Sure, those new trend and channel lines may need to be adjusted or corrected, but that is the information we now have. We now know there is major resistance at $59, there is resistance at $54, and we have a new lower low and a new lower high.

The stock is now below all the major moving averages and showing every sign of a classic market top. So we must either change our trading strategy or stay away from the market until it shows signs of strength. Buying dips only works in an advancing market unless you are trading very short term. And as you can see, the bounces are now only lasting a few days before a lower low hits. So realistically, buying dips in a declining market becomes very risky business.

Therefore, in a declining market, our strategy must change to trade with the primary trend of the market instead of against it. There have been many who tried to trade against the market, but few are ever successful. History teaches us that in market declines more than 80% of all stocks decline with the market.

Thus, picking the one or two stocks that might be advancing is like finding a needle in a haystack. And the other problem with that is, even the ones that have the strength to move against the prevailing trend usually do not advance very long. Eventually they will succumb to the selling pressure.

They can't fight the major trend for very long because eventually some traders will be forced to sell for whatever reason, maybe a margin call. When they are forced to sell, they will likely sell the stocks that are showing a profit, hoping the losers will eventually advance so they won't sustain a loss.

That is why there is no safe place to hide when the major market is in a decline. And that is the reason you must trade and invest with the major market trend and not against it.

# CHAPTER 19

## *Trading the Declines*

Trading in a declining trend requires either short-selling or buying put options. That way you are making money as the market falls to new lows.

Many people either do not like to sell short, or simply just don't know enough about it and are scared to do it. But in reality, selling short can reap much quicker profits than buying. (buying is referred to as entering a 'long position') The reason being, stocks fall faster than they rise. You will notice on all charts that when the market is advancing, it usually moves higher slowly in small increments. But a sell-off can be very rapid, especially when a stock breaks a support level. That is when the stop losses kick in and the orders are filled sending the prices lower very quickly.

Finding entry points to enter a short-sale trade is very similar to our entering the previous trade. The only difference is, we look for signs of weakness at the top instead of signs of strength at the bottom. In my book, **Trading the Trends**, I go into several short-sale trades in both stocks and options in declining markets to show how to find, enter, and manage those trades. But we will learn to find the setups here as well.

Just like any other trade, we start with the big picture. If you don't know where the stock has come from, you can't possibly know where it might go.

See Figure 21-1 below.

In the above chart we can see our stock was in an uptrend, broke that primary trend, has made a lower high, and has now traded back up to the new upper channel line. The 200 DMA is rolling over, the 50 DMA is headed down, and from all appearances it looks as if a new primary trend is in place.

We can see the stock has traded back above the 200 DMA but looks like it may be about to break below it once again. So let's take a closer look.
See Figure 21-2 below.

Let's look at a new developing picture. The new upper trend line was drawn from the highest high, connected to the high at $50 and then extended from there. We see the stock has traded right up to touch the trend, further confirming this new trend is valid. We also see the stock has traded back down below the 200 DMA and closed very close to it.

Notice the candles that are our early warning signals. There are two DOJIs, a spinning top that is located right at the peak of that high and then a confirming negative engulfing candle. There are at least three warnings that the current advance is about to change.

Most importantly, these warning candles formed at the top *after* an advance. The stock is trading at $47 and the last known support is at $44 per share. This is a low risk entry. By selling it short at $47, we can place a Buy Stop Loss at $48.50, just above the resistance. That way our maximum loss is $1.50 per share.

Remember, that is the key. We always buy at support, and if we are selling short, then we sell at resistance. So we are minimizing our loss and have a potential for a very nice gain.

Done! We have just sold short 500 shares of QQQ.

We are placing our Buy Stop Loss at $48.50 to protect our capital in the event we are wrong. A Buy Stop Loss will purchase the stock back and close the short sale trade if the stock trades up to our stop price. Thus, it will protect us from a major loss if the stock were to advance much higher.

Our maximum loss is $750, and even if the last known support at $44 holds, we can still make $3 per share.

However, we are entering this trade with the anticipation that the support will not hold. We can safely conclude this because we know the stock is weak and we know it is in a downtrend. Therefore, support levels are less likely to hold under these conditions. When selling tops, we are not concerned with support holding, we are concerned with resistance holding. This is exactly backwards from buying bottoms.

Let's see how our trade developed.

See Figure 21-3 below.

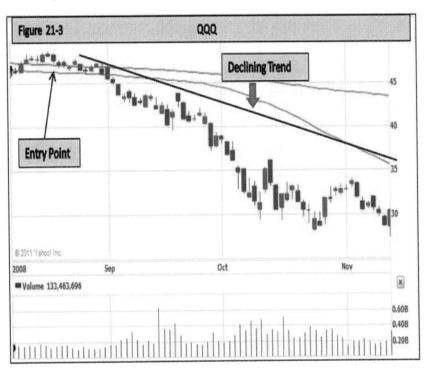

As you can see, the stock only paused briefly at the $44 support level. It is now trading around $30 per share which translates into a $17 gain for us. I think you can do the math on that one.

The point is, selling short can be very profitable. The entry points are found by looking for weakness and using technical analysis. The DOJIs, the Hanging Man, Spinning Tops, Engulfing candles and other known predictors that indicate a change is coming are found at the tops, *after* an advance, and that is key. When the market is declining, you are selling tops, not buying bottoms. So you must wait for a rally to a known resistance level, or, for it to trade up to a declining trend line.

That way you are selling at the top.

I know I don't have to remind you of this – but I will. Remember when we entered the first trade of this stock at $44.50?

Think about the buy-and-hold investor who purchased the stock at $44.50, didn't use a stop loss, and is still holding the stock. We exited the trade at, or near the top with a nice profit. Depending on your stop loss, you likely made at least $10 per share. And, for 500 shares, that translates into a $5,000 profit. Yet the buy-and-hold investor is now looking at the stock price trading at roughly $30 per share, and is seeing the loss of about $14 per share in his account. Thus, he is down about $7,000 from his original investment, plus, who knows if

$30 per share is the bottom... Just a reminder, using technical analysis and a stop loss will prevent a gain from turning into a loss.

# *Know the Difference*

Although we have covered a huge amount of information, I feel it is vitally important for you to know the difference in a good setup and a bad one. Meaning, there are times that patterns may form, certain candles may appear and you might think it is a good time to enter. There are times this will happen to all of us, but I want you to know how to possibly avoid the mistakes.

Let's look at a random chart and learn why you would not enter a trade. See Figure 21-4 below.

In the above chart, the stock has been in an uptrend to the high of about $51 and then sells off. A DOJI is formed on the second pullback. Why would this not be a good entry point?

1.  Look at the long wick on the big down day just seven days prior to the DOJI. That indicates there are sellers who are willing to sell at $4 below the DOJI price level.
2.  The known support is at $44 shown on the left side of the chart, that is $3 away, and the 50 DMA is only $1.50 above the current price. Not only is the 50 DMA just a $1.50 up above the current price, the stock has tried to trade above it once already and failed.
3.  The DOJI formed after only two negative trading days.

You see, a support level needs to be found, tested, and have more than one positive candle indicating a change is coming. A two-day decline is insignificant. You want to see a decline where the stock may have traded down for possibly 7 days, maybe longer, before you start to rely on indicators to predict what the next move will be. Remember in our earlier trade, the stock traded six days at support and then traded higher one day to confirm a likely advance. *Then* we entered the trade.

In this case, the 50 DMA is directly above the stock. You always need headroom, room for an advance, and there is none.

The point is, wait for a setup. They take time to develop. And they don't normally happen with one candle.

Let's look at another example of a bad setup.

See Figure 21-5 below.

Now we have a stock that has been in an uptrend and has seemingly found support at about $36.50 and traded there for almost 10 days. Realizing it is under the 50 DMA, would it be a buy now, or if it trades above the 50 DMA?

No.

1. We see there is known resistance, not only the 50 DMA but at $38. That is only a little over $1 away.
2. Support is at least $3 the other direction.
3. This low was made after just a three day decline.

Although there are spinning tops and positive candles indicating some strength, you want more headroom. If it were to trade down to the 200 DMA and then form some candles that were indicating it might advance, then it might be a good entry.

I used to have a rule of thumb that I often used. I would never buy a stock unless the DOW dropped at least 100 points. I still apply that rule occasionally. You see, in order to buy at a bottom, there must be a pullback. And the market moves in cycles, and these cycles usually are about three or five days advance and then a three or five day decline. If the market was in an uptrend, I would wait for a significant pullback before entering any long position. That way I placed as many odds in my favor as possible.

During a declining market, I would never short a stock or buy a put option unless there was about a five day rally. Even then I was hesitant to go short unless that rally ended close to a resistance level.

The point is, the chart patterns, the candles that historically prove to be great indicators, and moving averages are great. They work. But only if you do not try to read something into the chart that's not there.

Too many times a trader will see a DOJI form after a two or three day decline and assume that is a bottom. You must wait for the patterns to develop. When they do, you won't have to look for something that's not there. You will recognize it.

# CONCLUSION

Too many traders try to find the one magic indicator or signal that will always be successful. They try to use Bollinger Bands, Oscillators, Waves, and numerous other trading tools and gadgets. What they don't understand is, most every tool and gadget on the market is based in one way or the other on *price and volume*.

Probably more than half of the technical market indicators are oscillators of one kind or another, and I find oscillators highly overrated. I never use them.

Using them often encourages a person to put something more into the market than is really there. If you can't see what is happening in the market, you won't discover some deeper truth or magic trading secret by studying an oscillator.

Stick with the price and volume. It is all right there in the charts. We've all heard the phrase, "Follow the Money." The money on the table is what creates the charts in the first place. It does not lie to you like an analyst or talking head on TV will.

Remember that the market is just sometimes unpredictable. So instead of searching for some indicator that will tell you what you *want to hear*, wait for a chart pattern to develop that you recognize. Wait for a bottom to develop. Exercise patience at all times. The market isn't going anywhere; it will still be there tomorrow, and the next day.

If you miss an advance, there will be another on another day. So don't fret over the little things. Learn, and keep learning.

Starting out, don't get bogged down in the stochastics, waves, ratios, etc... Practice, and learn technical analysis, moving averages and always use a Stop Loss. They are easy, valuable, and they work. Remember, it is much easier to be successful as a long term investor or swing trader (Intermediate term). Day Trading requires minute by minute decisions and takes years to perfect. But by trend trading and swing trading, you can look at the overall market and the stocks you are interested in with a much better view. It is much easier to look at the bigger picture, longer term, and see the direction of the market as a whole and find good entry points in the current trading range based on the big picture.

Always remember to trade and invest **with** the market. The market is bigger than you are, it's bigger than any of us, and if you try to trade against it you will lose.

If you are a long term investor or trend trader, here is a simplified list of what you should check before every trade.

1)   Check a 2-year, 6-month, and 3-month chart on the company you are interested in.

2)   Check the overall market with the same charts. Make sure the general market is moving in your direction.

3)   Apply 50 and 200 DMA to the 2-year and 6-month charts.

4)   Apply 20 and 50 DMA to the 3-month chart.

5)   Then if you need to, use a 30-day chart to take a closer look at what is currently happening. You can even apply a 10 DMA on this one.

Make sure your potential stock or investment is headed in your direction.

**Listen to what the chart tells you – locate DOJIs, Hammers, Engulfing candles, Chart patterns, and implement them to your advantage.**

Wait for a chart pattern to develop that you recognize. If you don't recognize a pattern, then keep your money in your pocket until you do see one that you recognize.

What you are always looking at is the risk vs. reward ratio. Make sure you have the best possible opportunity for *small risk* with a potentially *high reward*. That is the difference technical analysis makes in your decisions. Without technical analysis it is a gamble, a crap shoot. But by applying time-tested chart patterns and knowledge, then the risk is greatly reduced, and it becomes an informed decision, not a gamble.

## Stop Loss

**I cannot emphasize strongly enough the importance
of a Stop Loss.**

Place a stop loss immediately after you place your trade.

In the event you are trading a security that a stop loss is
not available, then set an alert so you will know if the
price has dropped to your exit point. Then JUST DO IT!
Don't make excuses, or wait and see. Your exit point
must be determined *before* you purchase. Being *stopped
out* does not mean you placed a bad trade – It may only
mean the time was wrong. It may only mean the overall
market changed directions. Always minimize your
potential loss with this stop loss, but be realistic. In other
words, don't buy a stock for $25 and put a stop loss at
$24.50. Every stock has to have a little breathing room.
But always hold your potential losses to a minimum.

As your investment increases in value – move your stop
loss up. Continue to do this on increases in price using
technical analysis to locate new support and resistance
levels. This prevents having a sizable gain, and then
watching it vanish.

## Be Patient

Never pay much attention to the 'Talking Heads' on the
financial news networks. Their goal is only to
sensationalize trading and investing for rating purposes. I
am sure you can remember when the market was hitting

an all-time high, there were many so-called 'Gurus' professing their belief that the DOW would go to 20,000. And it certainly may some day. But as you know, it fell to 6600 instead of skyrocketing to 20,000.

So be patient, don't get in a hurry. Wait until you find an investment or trade that you feel comfortable with. Look for chart patterns that you recognize. Maybe even wait for a market correction to place your trade. As Baron Rothschild said, **"The time to buy is when there is blood in the streets."**

There are many old investors that will only buy after a market correction. Some will even wait years for the right opportunity to present itself. No, these individuals did not make much money from interest earned on holding their money in a bank. But they did not lose any of their money while trying to buy at the wrong time. So they sit on the sidelines and watch the market until they have a very low risk opportunity with the possibility of a very high rate of return.

There are many days the market is simply not tradable. Meaning, the market may have no direction. It may be trading sideways. It may be extremely volatile. So yes, there are many times it is better to keep your money in your pocket and watch from the sidelines. During these times you should do your research and look for opportunities to take advantage of when better market conditions are present.

We've discussed technical analysis as it is applied to the financial markets.

We've discussed the major tools utilized by the chartist, including: basic chart analysis, the study of volume, moving averages, and many aspects of technical analysis.

The successful trader/investor learns how to combine all these elements into one coherent theory of market analysis. The many software and Internet-based products available on the market today also provide powerful tools that make charting and technical analysis much easier and far more accessible to general investors than ever before.

Technical analysis provides an excellent vehicle for *market forecasting*, either with or without fundamental input. Where technical analysis becomes absolutely essential, however, is in the area of *market timing*. Market timing is purely technical in nature, so successful participation in the markets dictates some application of technical analysis.

It's not necessary to be an expert chartist to benefit from chart analysis. However, chart analysis will go a long way in keeping the trader on the right side of the market and in helping to pinpoint market entry and exit points, which are so vital to trading success.

*END*

I hope you have gained valuable insight and this book has been a learning experience. I look forward to sharing

trading and investing knowledge with you in the future.

## *Happy Trading*

## *Fred McAllen*

**Other Books by Fred McAllen:**

**Trading the Trends**

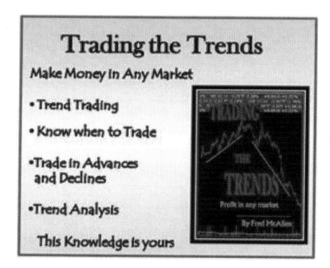

## *Common Sense Investing*

The Investing Book an
investor cannot do without.

Learn market history and
a common sense approach
To investing.
You will learn the good and
Bad about:
• Buy and Hold
• The Best Six Months Strategy
• Options Strategy
• Moving Average Strategy
•And Much More - -
Most of all, you will become a well informed
investor. A true learning experience.

## *The Inside Trader*

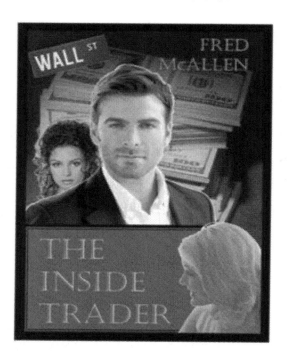

Although the story hinges on an insider trading scheme discovered by stockbroker, Carter Jackson, the real action is where his discovery takes him. The decisions he makes are crucial, and he must devise a plan to keep his money while avoiding fines, penalties, and possible jail time. Hiding money is not easy, but he finds a way, as his job, his marriage, and his stable life hang in the balance.

**"This is a really clever story that is so close to non-fiction I could easily see the potential in this becoming a film. I am really impressed with how Fred**

McAllen has managed to effortlessly incorporate corruption, mystery, romance and intrigue into this novel."
*E.R. Orchard, UK columnist*

*"The Inside Trader* is riveting from beginning to end. Fred McAllen blurs the line between reality and fiction with his character Carter Jackson. As the story unfolds you can't help but wonder what's going to happen next, this book has it all; intrigue, mystery, romance, corruption, and the depths of the characters make this an entertaining read and a real page-turner."
*Carter Lee, Columnist of In That Moment of Space for the Washington Times*

"A super read from start to finish - You won't be able to put it down!"
*~ Readers Chronicle*

Made in the USA
Columbia, SC
24 July 2021